DATE DUE

# MIGHTIER THAN THE SWORD

## Powerful Writing, In Class - On The Job

*Blue Jeans Press*
A division of LEL Enterprises
P.O. Box 5628
Charlottesville, VA 22905
(804) 293-7360
(800) 662-9673 (orders only)

# C. Edward Good

*Blue Jeans Press*
A division of LEL Enterprises
P.O. Box 5628
Charlottesville, VA 22905
(804) 293-7360
(800) 662-9673 (orders only)

ISBN 0-934961-02-6
*MIGHTIER THAN THE SWORD*
*Powerful Writing — In Class, On the Job*

*Beneath the rule of men entirely great*
*The pen is mightier than the sword.*

—Edward George Bulwer-Lytton
*Richelieu*, Act II, scene ii

# Dedication

For my junior high school English teachers,
Mary Frances Hazelman and Helen V. Hamrick,
whose dedication to our language
and strict insistence on correct expression
enriched the lives of thousands of children
in Greensboro, North Carolina.

# About the Author

C. Edward Good has devoted much of his professional career to teaching managers how to write clearly and persuasively and lawyers how to write not like lawyers. Mr. Good received his law degree from the University of Virginia in 1971. For five years, he taught writing to law students at the University of Virginia and to students at the Georgetown University Legal Assistant Program. Mr. Good was also selected to serve the Supreme Court of the United States and the Federal Judicial Center as a Tom C. Clark Judicial Fellow in 1977-78. Since 1980, he has presented seminars on persuasive writing to hundreds of managers and practicing attorneys in major cities across the country. Other than writing this book, his most ambitious and professionally rewarding project has been creating and conducting training programs in effective writing for 400 attorneys in the Associate Chief Counsel's Office of the Internal Revenue Service in Washington, D.C.—a project currently underway as this book goes to press.

Other professionals sponsoring Mr. Good's seminars include country club managers at the Club Managers Association of America, ex-cops at the Drug Enforcement Administration, engineers at the Federal Aviation Administration, economists at the Health Care Financing Administration, and top managers at the United States Postal Service.

To all the participants in these courses, Mr. Good expresses his gratitude, for they were the ones who taught the teacher most everything he knows.

# TABLE OF CONTENTS

# PREFACE

*Omne tulit punctum qui miscuit utile dulci,*
*Lectorem delectando pariterque monendo.*

He has gained every point who has mixed practicality with pleasure, by delighting the reader at the same time as instructing him.

—Horace

*Latina Sententia in libri capite elegantissima est.*

A Latin quotation at the chapter's front is cool.

—Good

# Preface

**Does your participle dangle?**

I'm a firm believer in grabbing the reader's attention right from the start. Did I grab yours? I hope so, for you must pay attention to what I have to say in this book. Why? Because many people in this country have a terrible time putting their thoughts down on paper. Writing—particularly writing well—has become a lost art. At least that's the opinion of 84 percent of the nation's Chief Executive Officers, who marked "inadequate writing skills" as their main concern about recent MBAs. *MBAs*. Not undergraduates. *MBAs*. Something must be wrong. Did television and some English teachers get in the way of clear expression?

Perhaps certain experiments in the 1960s and 1970s failed. Some teachers thought it'd be cool to downplay grammar. After all, who needs grammar? It's just a bunch of rules that'll get students all confused. Gets in the way of creativity. Causes all kinds of problems. Diagramming sentences? Are you kidding? That was stuff for the 1950s. Went out with the Edsel.

Guess what, folks, grammar's back. It's got to come back if people ever want to learn how to write. "And why is that?" you ask. Because it is impossible to analyze the quality of a person's writing without referring to grammar. "But isn't 'style' just a matter of opinion?" you ask. No. There's good style and bad style. To describe either intelligently, one must refer to the rules of grammar. "But when you say 'good style' or 'bad style,' that's just your opinion, isn't it?"

Yes.

Pick up some writing around you in your office or in your filing cabinet or even in a scholarly journal. Read it aloud. With a straight face. Can you read it once and understand it? Or does it require you to stop, scratch your head, wrinkle your brow, back up, and read it again? If you have to read it again, the writing isn't very good.

The writing I'm talking about, of course, is expository writing. The writing I'm writing about is the writing you see every day, the writing you write every day. It's the memo to the boss, the letter to the client, the term paper to the professor, and even the article in the journal. For lack of a true genre, let's just call it everyday writing, occupational writing, scholarly writing, or just plain old report writing. Whatever it is, this book seeks to help you do it a whale of a lot better than you do right now.

The style of this traditional writing is fairly predictable. Review some typical business writing in one part of the country and it will resemble that found a thousand miles away. Let's face it, if you've read one business report, you'll think you've read them all. Read some scholarly writing in one journal and it'll sound just like the writing in another. And, God forbid, make it through one government study and you can probably make it through any government study. The style you find in all is pretty much the same.

Because this style is predictable, its grammatical features can be identified and criticized. Many people, including the nation's CEOs, believe this typical style cries out for change. Others, no doubt, will cling to traditional ways of saying things. Those fearful of change might feel threatened. Writing simply, they think, is the same as thinking simply. "The subject matter of my profession is complex!" they point out. "The thinking in my profession is abstract," they say. "The substance I deal with is multifaceted," they reason. Therefore, writing about this tough stuff must be complex, abstract, multifaceted—in short, *hard*. If the message is tough, so too must be its medium.

Exactly the reverse is true. As information becomes more complex, writers should take greater care to present it in a simple way. If readers must strain to figure out highly complex sentences, replete with clauses and clauses within clauses, they will have little mental energy left over to deal with the message itself. Many of the great writers of our time knew this to be true. In the legal profession, for example, those judges known as good writers all favored simple styles. As a result, they were able to grab their readers' attention and lead them through the most difficult legal analysis. If at all, their readers would pause only to think about substance, not to fight their way through the fog of a cumbersome style.

The grammatical causes of a foggy style are easy to identify. Certain grammatical constructions actually hinder communication. Certain types of words get in the way of the message. Much professional jargon seeks to exclude the outsider. Once writers understand these constructions and see how they do indeed cloud communication—and ultimately lose arguments—they can, with practice, cut through the fog and develop instead a style that wins.

Some features of style are empirical. The number of words a writer uses, for example, is empirical. The number of sentences a writer uses is empirical. Dividing words by sentences yields an average sentence length, which is empirical. Study after study has shown that as average sentence length goes up, reader comprehension goes down.

Other features are also empirical. Stylists like Henry Fowler, William Strunk, and E. B. White knew the power of the short word. Fowler analyzed the writing in *Paradise Lost, The Idylls of the King,* and *The Bible* by calculating the percentage of monosyllabic words, finding in various passages 52 out of 56 and 89 out of 101. (Fowler, p. 344). Never one to mince his own words, Fowler took aim at the pedant and blasted away: "Those who run to long words are mainly the unskillful and tasteless; they confuse pomposity with dignity, flaccidity with ease, and bulk with force." (Fowler, p. 342). In a similar vein, Strunk & White advised: "Avoid the elaborate, the pretentious, the coy, and the cute. Do not be tempted by a twenty-dollar word when there is a ten-center handy, ready and able. Anglo-Saxon is a livelier tongue than Latin, so use Anglo-Saxon words." (Strunk & White, pp. 76-77).

Other features of a foggy style can be identified and analyzed. The main problems include writing with gaps, putting crucial information at subordinate parts of sentences, failing to use parallelism as a strategy (as I am now doing), using derivative nouns and adjectives to convey the meaning of verbs, preferring clauses over phrases, confusing restrictive and nonrestrictive clauses, misusing the verb *to be,* overusing the passive voice, and succumbing to his/hermaphrodism. His/her what? Nonsexist writing. More about that later.

Working in classes and individual sessions with hundreds of professionals, I have seen first hand the vast improvements writers can make in their writing styles. Initially my students are skeptical. They write like everyone else. How can there be a better way, they wonder. We've done it like this for years, they explain with satisfaction. Besides, they think, style is just a matter of opinion. No one can prove that one way of writing is necessarily better than another.

But then the light turns on. They begin to look at their writing in a new way. They learn to identify the predictable features of a foggy style. They begin to learn the grammatical names of those features. They start to think, believe it or not, about phrasing information with present participles and infinitives instead of derivative nouns. They slowly begin to see the connection between long-forgotten rules of grammar and the very real and current problem of writing a readable report.

All you need to improve your style dramatically is a clear understanding of some grammatical tricks that heighten the clarity of expression. Learning these tricks will not be easy. At times you will be frustrated, thinking you could forget about grammar after escaping from high school. Making the new way of writing a part of you—a part of your professional trademark—will require dedication and plain hard work. Daily practice and careful thought will mark your effort. But once you realize the close connection between your success in life and the quality of your writing, you will gladly abandon the foggy ways of the past and adopt instead a style that is simple, direct, forceful, and, as a result, effective.

Way back when, way back when you were young, your parents taught you that you are what you eat. Now you're big. Now you're in a profession. Now you're in college. Now you're a scholar. Now you're a government official. Now, as you read this book, you'll learn a completely different but equally vital truth:

As a professional/student/scholar/public servant, you are what you write.

---

*References*

H. Fowler, *Modern English Usage* (2d ed. 1965).

W. Strunk & E. White, *The Elements of Style* (3d ed. 1979).

# Chapter 1

# The Grammatical Nature of Style

*Mediocribus esse poetis*
*Non homines, non di, non concessere columnae.*

Not gods, nor men, nor even booksellers have put up with
poets' being second-rate.

—Horace

# Chapter 1

# The Grammatical Nature of Style

## Introduction

What's so good about good writing? Put the other way: what's so bad about bad writing? Is it really possible to analyze a person's writing, give it an *A*, and explain why it's superior to another person's writing? Can one review a paper, give it a *C*, and rationally describe its deficiencies?

These questions nagged at me when I took over the writing program at the University of Virginia School of Law in 1975. I knew that law students would not sit back, smile, and accept their *B's* and *C's* equably. Not without a fight. Not without some explanation showing them why their writing came up short.

I tried at first using those conclusory labels we were all familiar with in college. I could always put little helpful messages in the margins of the students' papers. I could point out that passages were "awkward." Or, more helpfully, I could conclude that a particular sentence was "wordy." Maybe I could even guide them away from "legalese." Predictably, these efforts failed.

I was faced with the task of figuring out exactly what was bad about bad writing and good about good writing. I learned very quickly that legal writing should be no different from other writing. The objectives of any expository writing are to inform, to instruct, to transfer information from one brain to another. And maybe to convince. While at Virginia, I slowly developed a list of rules that writers could follow to reach these objectives more easily. After five years at Virginia, I began my own consulting firm to provide training programs for lawyers and managers in the art of writing clearly and persuasively. I felt I knew why people write the way they do and how to help them change.

After I taught persuasive writing by lecturing to attorneys and managers in various parts of the country, several federal agencies commissioned me to present in-house training programs and to work individually with attorneys and upper-level executives. The most ambitious of these efforts was launched by the Internal Revenue Service. The IRS commissioned a series of 12 courses over three years to train nearly 400 attorneys in the art of persuasive writing. The program required me to review writing samples, write analyses of any problems detected, and meet with each person for a one-on-one feedback conference.

Needless to say, the labels of "wordy" or "awkward" wouldn't help these attorneys. Instead, I had to figure out what, if anything, was wrong with each paper submitted, articulate those problems, and attempt to rewrite the criticized passages. The experience gave me the chance to test my own theories of clear expression as well as those of Fowler, Strunk, White, and other experts. Also, the experience allowed me to see whether people who had written in a particular way for years could change or, indeed, would want to change the way they write. Of most importance, the experience enabled me to find out if a grammatical analysis of traditional style might be the most effective way of teaching clear expression.

The positive response by the IRS attorneys convinced me that grammatical theories of style do work. I learned that lawyers are open to change. They do want to write clearly. They emphatically want to win cases and arguments. I found that most attorneys, like most professionals everywhere, have forgotten rules of grammar, probably because those rules as taught to us in school were eminently forgettable. The attorneys did not *break* grammatical rules. They were not *un*grammatical. Instead, like most people, they never realized the close connection between rules of grammar and rules of style.

That's what you can expect in this book—a careful and, I hope, informative and, I hope, entertaining discussion of the *grammar* that makes good writing good and bad writing bad.

### The Nature of a Bad Writing Style

What does bad writing look like? Here's some:

> The original, duplicate and triplicate copies of the enclosed agreement should be signed and dated, as indicated, with the corporate name, followed by the signature of an authorized corporate officer or an authorized representative. After it has been executed in triplicate, the original and copies of this

agreement must be returned to this office within thirty days. If the signed original and copies of the agreement are not received by this office within thirty days, it will be assumed that you no longer desire to enter into a closing agreement and our files with respect to this matter will be closed without further action.

Now look at this:

Please sign and date the original and the two copies of the enclosed agreement. You should use the corporate name and follow it with the signature of an authorized corporate officer or authorized representative. After signing the agreement and the copies, please return them to this office within thirty days. If we do not receive them within that time, we will assume that you no longer want to enter into a closing agreement and, accordingly, will close our files on this matter without further action.

What's the difference? Did the writer just rewrite the passage to make it sound simpler and more direct? Yes, but how? The writer recognized immediately that the original passage appeared exclusively in the passive voice. In the rewritten passage, the writer used the active voice. The writer also wanted to avoid words like *triplicate* and *execute* and to use instead simpler words like *two copies* and *sign.* The writer reduced the passage from 104 words to 85 words. The average sentence length dropped from 35 to 21. The number of polysyllabic words dropped from 44 to 31. Finally, the writer trashed the compound preposition *with respect to* and substituted the simple preposition *on.*

I'll let you decide about the next example, which, ironically, is discussing ways to teach people how to write. It was presented at a meeting of the Modern Language Association:

As I see it, basic writing theory will study two kinds of phenomena. One kind pertains to structures of mature discourse competence, the other to the developmental sequence traversed by learners in acceding to mature competence. The first implies investigation of the product of learning, the second research on the process of its acquisition. More specifically, inquiry into discourse competence will aim to develop a system and a nomenclature (i.e., a theory) characterizing the ideational structure of discourse—its semantic connectedness, so to speak—in hierarchical ways that bridge the large and almost totally uncharted gap between the level whereon intra-proposi-

tional word-to-word relations are studied by the generative
semanticist, and the whole-discourse level whereon the
rhetorician classifies separate discourse types. (*Quoted in* Kolb,
p. 42).

## The Nature of a Good Writing Style

Even lawyers have been known to produce some terrific writing.
Here's what Mr. Justice Black had to say about the First Amendment:

> Since the earliest days philosophers have dreamed of a
> country where the mind and spirit of man would be free; where
> there would be no limits to inquiry; where men would be free
> to explore the unknown and to challenge the most deeply rooted
> beliefs and principles. Our First Amendment was a bold effort
> to adopt this principle—to establish a country with no legal
> restrictions of any kind upon the subjects people could inves-
> tigate, discuss and deny. The Framers knew, better perhaps
> than we do today, the risks they were taking. They knew that
> free speech might be the friend of change and revolution. But
> they also knew that it is always the deadliest enemy of tyranny.
> With this knowledge they still believed that the ultimate happi-
> ness and security of a nation lies in its ability to explore, to
> change, to grow and ceaselessly to adapt itself to a new
> knowledge born of inquiry free from any kind of governmental
> control over the mind and spirit of man. Loyalty comes from
> love of good government, not fear of a bad one. (Black, pp.
> 880-81).

Let's give Mr. Justice Black an *A* for the following reasons: (1) he
used 182 words in seven sentences, which yields an average sentence
length of 26 words per sentence; (2) he used 126 monosyllabic words, a
ratio of 66 percent; (3) he used zero compound prepositions; (4) he used
zero passive voice constructions; (5) he used only three -*ion* words; (6)
he used zero *which* clauses; (7) he used only three *that* clauses; (8) he
separated the subject from the verb in only two of the seven sentences;
and (9) he used 14 parallel constructions.

By grammatically analyzing Mr. Justice Black's style, we can explain our decision to award an *A*. Grammar, therefore, is not some set
of obscure rules leering over your shoulder, like your English teacher
of yore, poised to pounce when you make the slightest mistake. Grammar is not a source of dread. Instead, the vast array of grammatical

structures is your arsenal of weapons. Learn them—as you will in this book—and you can make grammar work for you. You can use grammar to spot the weaknesses in your current style and figure out ways to improve it.

### The Right Kind of Grammar

At this stage in my *Mightier than the Sword Seminar*, I usually warn the students:

> Get ready. We are about to take a trip down bad-memory lane. You are about to be bombarded with long-forgotten rules of grammar. Fear not, however, for I will assume your knowledge of grammar is not broad and deep, but thin and shallow

My assumption is usually correct. Though the vast majority of students, scholars, and professionals write grammatically, they do not *think* in grammatical terms. By that I mean this: people who *write for a living* have a natural feel for the language. They have grown up in grammatical households or overcome their ungrammatical upbringings by dedicated hard work. They do not make many grammatical mistakes. If they hear or see a grammatical mistake, they can identify it as such. But they might have a little trouble explaining the precise nature of the mistake.

The question naturally arises: must you become an expert grammarian before you can possibly be an excellent writer? The answer is an emphatic "no." Next question: can you identify your problems in writing without referring to grammar at all? A more emphatic "no." We seek instead a middle ground. To become a better writer, you must know enough grammar and the right kind of grammar.

"The right kind of grammar?" you ask.

For the past 17 years, I have studied writing from a unique perspective. I have been asked by hundreds of students, lawyers, and other professionals to explain what is wrong with their writing. I have tried to explain style in terms of style and found such an approach totally fruitless. When I shifted my focus and explained style in terms of grammar, I saw the students respond.

"But what grammar?" you ask. "I know all about subject-verb agreement. I never confuse the case of pronouns. And, no, my participles don't dangle. Just exactly what do you mean 'the right kind of grammar'?"

As mentioned in the Preface to this book, stuffy, foggy writing is predictable and definable. Certain structures characterize such writing as typical *professional-sounding* writing. When those structures are analyzed grammatically, the writer can begin to see why they do not do the job as effectively as others. These structures of typical expository writing involve certain basic but often complicated rules of grammar.

The *right kind of grammar* thus includes those rules that keep popping up when one analyzes typical writing found in college, academe, government, or business. For example, because most writers tend to prefer the passive voice, the *right kind of grammar* includes an extensive discussion of transitive and intransitive verbs and the differences between the active voice and the passive voice. Because writers favor tangles of clauses, the *right kind of grammar* includes a careful study of adjective, adverb, and noun clauses. Because writers adore stuffy noun forms—a condition known as *nouniness*—the *right kind of grammar* will explore derivative nouns and derivative adjectives and instruct you in the proper use of verb forms.

Looked at the other way, plenty of rules of grammar just don't even come up when analyzing typical expository writing. For example, such writing rarely displays problems of subject-verb agreement. Thus, noticeably absent from the *right kind of grammar* is any discussion whatsoever of plural subjects and plural verbs.

This book seeks to teach you the grammatical principles that make good writing good and bad writing bad. By learning to recognize these grammatical attributes of clear writing, you will learn to use them to increase your power as a writer, to influence other people through the written word, and perhaps even to think in a different and clearer way.

At a minimum you will learn why some writers get an *A* and most writers don't.

*References*

H. Black, *The Bill of Rights,* 35 N.Y.U. L. Rev. 865, 880-81 (1960).

H. Kolb, *A Writer's Guide* (1980).

# Chapter 2

# The English Sentence

*Dixeris egregie notum si callida verbum*
*Reddiderit iunctura novum.*

You will have written exceptionally well if, by skillful
arrangement of your words, you have made an ordinary
one seem original.

—Horace

# Chapter 2

## The English Sentence

### Introduction

We begin our search for clarity in style by looking carefully at the English sentence. Not surprisingly, if you have trouble writing, chances are good you are breaking some very basic rules on constructing effective sentences. Understanding these basic rules and seeing what happens when you break them are indispensable first steps along the road to clarity.

That road begins by backing up to grade school and studying the four basic structures of English sentences. With those structures firmly in mind, you will then see the important relationship between sentence structure and *sentence length*. The *not-too-many-thoughts-per-sentence rule* will make a great deal of sense. A basic rule—*the subject-predicate = main message rule*—will guide the ordinary structure of your sentences. For variety and emphasis, you will learn the *art of inversion*. To avoid choppiness, you will learn the *art of subordination*. You will appreciate the *rule against gaps* and see how and why many writers routinely ignore it. You will recall the *grammatical rule of parallelism* and see how the best writers use the rule to their advantage. You will see how to use *tabulation* to handle particularly complex information.

Having mastered the intricacies of effective sentence-building, you will then be ready to learn the ways of choosing the right word, working powerfully with verbs, using nouns effectively, and paring it all down into a nice, tight package.

### Some Preliminary Rules of Grammar

Before we get to the four basic ways you can build the English sentence, you must first recall three bits of grammar: (1) the difference between *transitive* and *intransitive verbs*, (2) the nature of the verb *to be*, and (3) the nature of *linking verbs*. Though we'll return to the effective use of verbs throughout this book, for now you should ponder their nature and the basic ways they work in our language.

### The Difference Between Transitive and Intransitive Verbs

Transitive Verb: A transitive verb is an action verb that has a direct object. An action verb is transitive if it can be followed immediately by a noun that receives the action from the verb. Thus: *The corporate communications department prepared the annual report.* The verb *prepared* is transitive because it is capable of having a noun immediately follow it. The direct object *report* receives the action of the transitive verb.

Intransitive Verb: An intransitive verb, on the other hand, is not followed immediately by a noun. Indeed, an intransitive verb yearns not for a noun but for an adverb. Thus: *The employee complied with the personnel policy.* The verb *complied* is intransitive because it cannot be followed immediately by a noun. It can have no direct object at all.

You can test the *transitiveness* of a verb by answering this question: *Can I [verb] something or somebody?* Plug in the verb and answer the question. If the answer is "yes," the verb is transitive. If the answer is "no," the verb is intransitive. Apply the test to the two verbs above. Can I *prepare* something? Yes, I can prepare a report or prepare some plans. *Prepare* is transitive. Can I *comply* something? No. I can only comply *with* something. *Comply* is intransitive.

Many people incorrectly think that all action verbs are transitive verbs. Well, some are and some aren't. Some action verbs have dual meanings, a transitive one and an intransitive one. Take the action verb *to walk*, for example. Test it. Can I *walk* something or somebody? Ordinarily not. I don't walk *something* [noun]. Instead, I walk *where* [adverb], *how* [adverb], *why* [adverb], or *when* [adverb]. Thus, I walk *to the store* [adverbial prepositional phrase]. I walk *quickly* [adverb]. I walk *for exercise* [adverbial prepositional phrase]. Or I walk *during the evening* [adverbial prepositional phrase]. As a rule, I do not walk *something* or *somebody*. The verb *to walk*, therefore, is intransitive. If I take my dog along, however, the verb becomes transitive. Thus, I walk *my dog* to the store. Now I've got the direct object *dog* receiving the action of the transitive verb *walk*.

Later, we will return to study transitive verbs at some length when we examine the crucial rules governing the active and passive voice.

### The Nature of the Verb "To Be"

Though there are a few exceptions, as a rule the verb *to be* will be followed either by an adjective (predicate adjective) or a noun (predicate nominative or subject complement). Thus: *These issues are pertinent to our inquiry. Pertinent* is the predicate adjective following the verb *are* and describing the subject of the sentence *issues*. Or: *The decision was a landmark case in the area of employee relations. Case* is the predicate nominative (also called the *subject complement*) following the verb *was* and restating or defining the subject of the sentence *decision*.

### The Nature of Linking Verbs

In addition to transitive verbs, intransitive verbs, and the verb *to be*, the English language includes another verb form, the linking verb. A linking verb is really a surrogate for the verb *to be*. It "links" the subject of the sentence to an adjective in the predicate position, that is, following the verb.

The most common linking verbs include the following: *seem, appear, feel,* and *look.* Thus: *He seems ill. He appears quick. He feels bad. He looks defeated.*

Please note that these verbs link the subjects of sentences to adjectives, not adverbs. Indeed, if you follow a linking verb with an adverb, you will say some rather weird things because the adverb must modify the verb: "He feels badly" means his tactile ability is deficient. Also, a linking verb, particularly in England, might link the subject to a noun: *He seems an honest man.*

### Four Basic Sentence Structures

Every English sentence must have a grammatical subject (a noun or a noun form) and a conjugated verb. The conjugated verb might also be called the *predicate verb.* A conjugated verb can form a sentence—an independent clause. It can also form a dependent clause. (For simplicity, I am going to refer to the conjugated verb as the *main verb,* whether it appears in an independent clause or a dependent clause.) Each sentence will have, at least, one grammatical subject and one main verb. Thus, right off the bat, you can see two "biggies" in the typical sentence: the subject and the main verb. Sentences have a third "biggie," however. The third part will be determined by the main verb. If the main verb is transitive, the third part of the sentence will be the direct object—if the sentence appears in the active voice. However, if the sentence appears in the passive voice, the third part might be a prepositional phrase revealing the actor. (We'll study the *voice* of transitive verbs in great detail in Chapter 7.) If the main verb is intransitive, the third part typically will be an adverb or adverbial phrase. If the main verb is the verb *to be*, the third part will be a predicate adjective or a predicate nominative. And, finally, if the main verb is a linking verb, the third part will be a predicate adjective. Thus, the four basic structures of the English sentence look like this:

1. Subject (actor) + Transitive Verb (active) + Direct Object (recipient)
   *Example: The school board punished the student.*

   Subject (recipient) + Transitive Verb (passive) + Phrase (actor)
   *Example: The student was punished by the school board.*

2. Subject + Intransitive Verb + Adverb
   *Example: Thereafter, the student complied with the policy.*

3. Subject + To Be + Predicate Adjective
   *Example: At first, the student was arrogant.*

   Subject + To Be + Predicate Nominative
   *Example: The student was the first offender of the new regulations.*

4. Subject + Linking Verb + Predicate Adjective
   *Example: When caught, the student felt terrible.*

   The English sentence, therefore, has three milestones: the subject, the main verb, and the other stuff. Readers anticipate this three-part structure. They expect to find these three parts of the sentence. They know to look for them. They want them to be the most important parts of the sentence. They know that other parts of the sentence are less important or "subordinate." Your readers expect these messages:

1. Who or What (subject) Does What (transitive verb in active voice) To What or To Whom (direct object)

   Who or What (subject) *Was Done To* (transitive verb in passive voice) By What or By Whom (actor)

2. Who or What (subject) Does What (intransitive verb) How or Where or When or Why (adverb)

3. Who or What (subject) Is (verb *to be*) Who or What (predicate nominative)

   Who or What (subject) Is (verb *to be*) What Kind or What Character or What Size, etc. (predicate adjective)

4. Who or What (subject) Seems or Feels (linking verb) What Kind or What Character or What Size, etc. (predicate adjective)

One-Two-Three. That's the basic, three-part structure of the English sentence. One-Two-Three. That's the message your readers expect to hear. And, as we'll soon see, this basic, three-part structure dictates many rules of style and provides several tests you may use to measure the quality of your writing.

### Average Sentence Length

If stylists agree on one thing, they agree on a rather basic rule: the average sentence length of effective writing will not exceed 30 words per sentence. The ideal average, for some unknown reason, is 25 words per sentence.

Recall the passage by Mr. Justice Black in Chapter 1 exploring the nature of the First Amendment. For your convenience, here it is again:

> Since the earliest days philosophers have dreamed of a country where the mind and spirit of man would be free; where there would be no limits to inquiry; where men would be free to explore the unknown and to challenge the most deeply rooted beliefs and principles. Our First Amendment was a bold effort to adopt this principle—to establish a country with no legal restrictions of any kind upon the subjects people could investigate, discuss and deny. The Framers knew, better perhaps than we do today, the risks they were taking. They knew that free speech might be the friend of change and revolution. But they also knew that it is always the deadliest enemy of tyranny. With this knowledge they still believed that the ultimate happiness and security of a nation lies in its ability to explore, to change, to grow and ceaselessly to adapt itself to a new knowledge born of inquiry free from any kind of governmental control over the mind and spirit of man. Loyalty comes from love of good government, not fear of a bad one.

The passage contains seven sentences having the following number of words: 47, 31, 14, 13, 13, 51, and 13. The total is 182. The average is 26. Did Mr. Justice Black know what he was doing? Or did he just write that way? Believe me. He knew exactly what he was doing. He knew the power of variety and varied his sentence length from a low of 13 to a high of 51. He knew the emphasis of isolation and surrounded his long sentences with short ones. He knew the value of repetition and willingly used the same verb (*knew*) as the main verb of three consecutive sentences. (I just copied him and used the same main verb in four consecutive sentences.) When building long sentences, the first and the sixth, he understood the need for an easily recognized structure and chose repetitive parallel forms to help the reader stay on track.

In short, he broke his information down into digestible bites, spoon-feeding his reader one bite at a time. He avoided the stuffy style of cramming the whole loaf down the reader's throat all at once.

You too should break down your information. You too should go right now to your files and fish out a sample of your writing. You too should get out your abacus or solar-powered calculator and tally the total of your words. You too should count the total number of your sentences. Then divide words by sentences to produce an average sentence length. If it's over thirty, you're in big trouble. You suffer from Long-Winded Sentence Syndrome, a malady afflicting many writers in most professions.

The causes are two. Either you cram too many messages into one sentence or you cram too many words into one message. The first cause is easy to cure. The second—wordiness—signifies a host of problems, which will occupy us for much of the remainder of this book.

Let's deal with the easily curable problem: trying to stuff a two-week vacation in an overnight bag. I'll abandon that metaphor now—or I'll never get out of it—and state the rule another way.

### The Not-Too-Many-Thoughts-Per-Sentence Rule

Everyone reading this book has written, at one time in their lives, a never-ending sentence. You know the kind. Somehow you get started with an idea, but suddenly that idea has all sorts of qualifications, which seem to fit only within the same sentence. So, what the heck, why not just continue. The reader can read it several times and figure it out.

Besides, we think, expressing ourselves with these long sentences is cool. At least they'll impress our boss, our client, our professor, or our date. Wrong. Long sentences don't impress anyone. All they do is confuse. Long-winded sentences are avoided like the plague by careful, effective writers.

I can best demonstrate the rule by showing its flagrant violation. Here's a passage analyzing some of the effects of false advertising. It has 80 words in one sentence. It crams a three-week cruise in a rowboat:

> While there are instances in which consumer abuse and exploitation result from advertising which is false, misleading, or irrelevant, it does not necessarily follow that these cases need to be remedied by governmental intervention into the marketplace because of the fact that it is possible for consumers' interests to be protected through resort to the courts, either by consumers themselves or by those competing sellers who see their market shares decline in the face of inroads based on such advertising. (*Quoted in* Wydick, pp. 38-39).

Here the writer broke the *not-too-many-thoughts-per-sentence rule*. He tried to cram all he had to say in a single sentence. Instead, he should have identified each major message and devoted a single sentence to each message. The mental process of identifying individual messages looks like this: (1) false advertising abuses consumers, (2) the government need not intervene in the marketplace, and (3) consumers can protect themselves as can sellers. By breaking the information down into digestible bites, the writer can then present each message to the reader in a single sentence:

> Consumers are sometimes abused by false, misleading, or irrelevant advertising. To cure the problem, however, the government need not intervene in the marketplace. Consumers can protect their own interests by going to court as can competing sellers who lose business because of such advertising. (See Wydick, p. 69).

The revised passage has 44 words in three sentences. The average length is just under 15 words per sentence. The thoughts are broken down into a manageable size that makes the passage easy to understand and to read. (The revised passage also uses many techniques we'll review later in the book to solve the problem of wordiness.)

Another way to follow the *not-too-many-thoughts-per-sentence rule* is the Stop-Start approach to writing. Writers often get started in a sentence and, for some reason, refuse to stop. They keep on going, adding message upon message on the back of a single sentence. Sooner, not later, the sentence collapses of its own weight, as does the patience of the reader.

The trick is to Stop at the end of one main message and to Start at the beginning of the next. Simply Stop the sentence with a period. Then Start the next with a capital letter. It's often that simple. Here's an example:

> The basis of the depreciable property consisting of selected assets as described in the schedule of selected assets contained in the Assistant Commissioner's letter dated 20 November 1979, from the machinery and equipment operated by the companies that are on hand as of December 31, 1979, shall be reduced by 100 percent of the income realized from the purchase of such debentures.

The writer of this passage fails to identify the three main messages: (1) the assets are described in the letter; (2) the assets include certain property; and (3) the basis of the assets shall be reduced. Instead, the writer continues and continues and continues, heaping thought upon thought upon thought. The better approach is to Stop. Then Start. Stop. Start. Stop. Here's how:

> The depreciable property includes property described in the schedule of selected assets in the Commissioner's letter of November 20, 1979. Specifically, this property includes the companies' machinery and equipment on hand as of December 31, 1979. The basis of this property shall be reduced by 100 percent of the income realized from the purchase of such debentures.

In sum, break your information down into digestible bites. Each bite should be a main message, which should appear in a single sentence. Use the Stop-Start device to kick the habit of cramming all your information down your reader's throat in a single, long-winded sentence. Your reader will appreciate the effort. Your reader won't choke.

## The Subject-Predicate = Main Message Rule

Recall the four basic sentence structures. Here they are again:

1. Subject (actor) + Transitive Verb (active) + Direct Object (recipient)
   *Example: The school board punished the student.*
   Subject (recipient) + Transitive Verb (passive) + Phrase (actor)
   *Example: The student was punished by the school board.*
2. Subject + Intransitive Verb + Adverb
   *Example: Thereafter, the student complied with the policy.*
3. Subject + To Be + Predicate Adjective
   *Example: At first, the student was arrogant.*
   Subject + To Be + Predicate Nominative
   *Example: The student was the first offender of the new regulations.*
4. Subject + Linking Verb + Predicate Adjective
   *Example: When caught, the student felt terrible.*

As a rule, you should identify your main message and position it at the subject-predicate position in the sentence. When reviewing your writing, you should pick out your subjects, your main verbs, and the other stuff (direct object, adverb, predicate adjective, or predicate nominative). You should then read this three-part structure aloud. Listen to your message and be sure it makes sense. These three parts in most of your sentences should carry most of your messages. They should inform. If, when you read these three vital parts of your sentences, you find very little information, you are probably suffering from the Thomas Paine Syndrome. You remember him from History 101. He was that famous American revolutionary who wrote:

These are the times that try men's souls.

Let's test the sentence against the *subject-predicate = main message rule*. The subject is *These*. The main verb is *are*. The predicate nominative is *times*. *These are times*. Not much there, huh? No, Paine subordinated his main message in the dependent clause: *that try men's souls*. Had he followed the rule, here's what he would have written:

These times try men's souls.

In these times, men's souls are tried.

Neither of those would have stirred the hearts of the colonists. Paine knew what he was doing. For emphasis he intentionally broke the *subject-predicate = main message rule*. By forcing his main message to the end of his sentence, by delaying his main message, he created tension in his reader. He created an exclamation point. He used the spice of our language.

Many writers, perhaps fancying themselves to be modern-day Thomas Paines, put very little information at the subject-verb-other-stuff structure of the sentence. Instead, they subordinate everything to dependent clauses and phrases. They dump way too much spice on their words, try to emphasize everything, and end up emphasizing nothing. They write like this:

> There are several procedures involved, which, if there is to be an increase in corporate income, must be carefully followed.

The subject? *There.* The main verb? *Are.* The predicate nominative? *Procedures.* Folks, I can now announce for the first time in history (a drum roll please):

THERE ARE PROCEDURES!

What a letdown. Here the writer is using the crucial, drum-rolling part of a sentence for naught. Instead, identify the message: (1) What, (2) Must what, (3) Why. (1) What [procedures], (2) Must what [must be followed], (3) Why [to increase corporate income]. One-two-three. That's the way most messages break down in the English language. We should therefore use the English language to say precisely what we mean:

> Several procedures must be carefully followed to increase corporate income.

To write powerfully, look at your subjects, look at your main verbs, and look at the other stuff. Read those three parts aloud. If you say very little, your writing is breaking the *subject-predicate = main message rule*. You are abandoning the most important parts of the English sentence. Use those parts for most of your messages. When it's time to drive a point home or vary your style, then play Thomas Paine or use other well-recognized ways to break the pattern.

### The Art of Inversion

If your writing becomes predictable, your reader will become bored. Every now and then you need to change the rules on your reader, to mix things up a bit, to break the pattern of the way you say things. One way to achieve highly desirable variety in your language is to invert the ordinary order of a sentence. Here's the way inversion can work for you.

The grammatical subject is at the front of the English sentence. (Or should I say: *At the front of the English sentence is the grammatical subject.*) The main verb is after the subject in the English sentence. (Or should I say: *After the subject in the English sentence is the main verb.*) The other stuff comes at the end. (Or should I say: *At the end comes the other stuff.*) You have just witnessed the art of inversion. I began each of the three parenthetical sentences above with the "other stuff." I then stated the main verb. Finally, at the end of the sentence, I positioned the subject.

In formal writing, the inverted sentence works well with the verb *to be.* Especially when describing factual events or settings, you should consider inversion as a particularly effective tool. Thus, instead of saying, *A large bush was to the driver's right and partially obstructed the view*, try inverting the sentence like this: *To the driver's right was a large bush, partially obstructing the view.* Changing the ordinary order of sentences grabs your reader's attention. Without knowing why, your reader becomes glued to your words.

Although you may invert sentences having verbs other than the verb *to be*, you should be very careful. You might succumb to the Grandmother's House Syndrome.

> Over the river and through the woods, to Grandmother's house we go.

Worse, if you invert too many sentences, you might fall prey to the Real Estate Classified Ad Syndrome:

> Nestled in this wooded lot is this three-bedroom charmer. Happy will be the day . . . .

Later in this book, you'll learn how to play around with positioning the actor of your sentences by switching the voice of your transitive verbs from the active to the passive.

### The Art of Subordination

I have taught persuasive writing to scores of students, executives, educators, and lawyers. Invariably, when they begin to adapt their styles to the rules of clear writing, they tend to overdo it a bit and produce sentences that are too short and choppy. To help them find a balance between the short, choppy style and the long-winded style, I always suggest the art of subordination as the cure.

Each English sentence has one of the four basic structures we discussed above. For convenience, here they are again:

1. Subject (actor) + Transitive Verb (active) + Direct Object (recipient)
   *Example: The school board punished the student.*

   Subject (recipient) + Transitive Verb (passive) + Phrase (actor)
   *Example: The student was punished by the school board.*

2. Subject + Intransitive Verb + Adverb
   *Example: Thereafter, the student complied with the policy.*

3. Subject + To Be + Predicate Adjective
   *Example: At first, the student was arrogant.*

   Subject + To Be + Predicate Nominative
   *Example: The student was the first offender of the new regulations.*

4. Subject + Linking Verb + Predicate Adjective
   *Example: When caught, the student felt terrible.*

Although I oversimplify somewhat, to these basic structures you may add only two things: adjectives and adverbs. These adjectives and adverbs might come in single-word form or multi-word form. If they come in multi-word form, they are either phrases or clauses. Phrases, you might recall, are defined as follows: *a bunch of words without a main verb in it.* Clauses, of course, are defined as follows: *a bunch of words with a main verb in it.* This book will deal at some length with phrases and clauses when we tackle problems of wordiness.

The four structures above are the strategic parts of the English sentence. All other parts—those containing adjectives, adverbs, adjective phrases, adverb phrases, adjective clauses, and adverb clauses—are *subordinate* parts of the sentence. Above we saw the general rule of placing your main message at the strategic part of the sentence. By the same token, a general rule requires that you place subordinate information at subordinate parts of the sentence.

The art of subordination requires you to recognize subordinate information in a separate sentence and put it in a nearby sentence containing more important information. Let's see how the art of subordination might smooth out the short, choppy sentences of a child:

> I like my teacher.
>
> My teacher is handsome.
>
> My teacher's name is Mr. Jones.

Using *handsome* as a subordinate, one-word adjective and *Mr. Jones* as a subordinate appositive (a noun restating another noun), the subordinated sentence looks like this:

> I like my handsome teacher, Mr. Jones.

Leaving grade school behind and moving up the scale of complexity, let's look at two other sentences crying out for subordination:

> Smith's employment was terminated by the Board. The Board relied on its conflict of interest policy in reaching this decision.

If you have trouble distinguishing the subordinate message from the strategic message, ask Smith. He'll tell you. The subordinate message is the Board's *relying on its conflict of interest policy*. The strategic message, of course, is Smith's getting the boot. Using the art of subordination, we produce this:

> Relying on its conflict of interest policy, the Board terminated Smith's employment.

The subordinate message appeared as an introductory present participial phrase. It acted as an adjective. It modified *Board*. Or should I say: The subordinate message appeared as an introductory present participial phrase acting as an adjective and modifying *Board*. Somehow I like the second, *subordinated* way better.

When you overdo it in your efforts to be brief, consider subordination as the ideal cure to choppiness. Of course, you might overdo it in your efforts to subordinate. You might put *strategic* information in subordinate positions. Or you might break the *not-too-many-thoughts-per-sentence rule* and try to cram too much information into subordinate parts of your sentences. If you do, the inevitable result is *gaps*, the great thought-stoppers in expository writing.

### Avoiding Gaps

Recall the sample passage by Mr. Justice Black in Chapter 1. The passage had seven sentences. In only two of those sentences was the subject separated from the verb by other words. Only two sentences had *gaps*. And, if you'll go back and study the passage, you'll see that the gaps between subject and verb were one-word adverbs.

Here's another well-known judge describing the bizarre facts in a well-known case, *Palsgraf v. Long Island Railroad*:

> Plaintiff was standing on a platform of defendant's railroad after buying a ticket to go to Rockaway Beach. A train stopped at the station, bound for another place. Two men ran forward to catch it. One of the men reached the platform of the car without mishap, though the train was already moving. The other man, carrying a package, jumped aboard the car, but seemed unsteady as if about to fall. A guard on the car, who had held the door open, reached forward to help him in, and another guard on the platform pushed him from behind. In this act, the package was dislodged and fell upon the rails. It was a package of small size, about fifteen inches long, and was covered by a newspaper. In fact, it contained fireworks, but there was nothing in its appearance to give notice of its contents. The fireworks when they fell exploded. The shock of the explosion threw down some scales at the other end of the platform many feet away. The scales struck the plaintiff, causing injuries for which she sues. (*Palsgraf*, p. 99).

In those twelve sentences, Mr. Justice Cardozo kept subject close to main verb. Let's test the twelve sentences for gaps: (1) plaintiff was standing (no gap); (2) train stopped (no gap); (3) men ran (no gap); (4) one of the men reached (three-word prepositional phrase); (5) man, carrying a package, jumped (three-word present participial phrase); (6) guard on the car, who had held the door open, reached (three-word prepositional phrase and six-word nonrestrictive clause); (7) package was dislodged (no gap); (8) it was (no gap); (9) it contained (no gap); (10) fireworks when they fell exploded (three-word adverb clause); (11) shock of the explosion threw (three-word prepositional phrase); and (12) scales struck (no gap).

Cardozo strictly limited those situations where strategic parts of sentences were pulled apart to allow other words to come in between. That's a gap. In only five sentences did he permit gaps. Four of those five were mere three-word gaps. The longest stretched only to nine words. Good writers avoid gaps. You should too.

The English sentence prefers strategic parts to remain close together. Your reader is looking for these milestones in your sentences. By disrupting ordinary patterns with thought-stopping gaps, you only baffle and irritate your reader.

Above we saw how Mr. Justice Cardozo limited gaps between subject and verb. Here's what a subject-verb gap looks and sounds like:

> This *office*, after a thorough review of its policies and proce- dures, a complete consideration of the ramifications of this decision, and an assessment of the performance which you have made from the commencement of your employment to the present time, *has made* the determination that your services will no longer be needed.

Gaps disrupt other strategic sentence parts as well. You will likely encounter gaps between parts of a complex verb, between a verb and its object, between the parts of an infinitive, and between *that* and the balance of a dependent clause.

### Between parts of a complex verb

Before I show an example of the complex verb gap, perhaps a quick review of grammar is in order. Remember verb conjugation? You conjugate verbs to show tense or time. A conjugated verb is a *predicate verb* used in an independent or dependent clause. As mentioned above, to make things simple, I call these conjugated verbs *main verbs*. The 12 major tenses of main verbs include: present, past, future, present per- fect, past perfect, future perfect and six progressive tenses. Only two tenses—present and past—can be shown with one-word verbs. Thus: *he writes* (present) and *he wrote* (past). All other tenses require *helping verbs*, also known as *auxiliary verbs*, to show the precise time when something happens. Thus: *he will write* (future), *he has written* (present perfect), *he had written* (past perfect), and *he will have written* (future perfect). Six additional tenses, the progressive tenses, allow us to show ongoing actions. All progressive tenses require the use of *to be* as an auxiliary verb: *he is writing* (present progressive), *he was writing* (past progressive), *he will be writing* (future progressive), *he has been writing* (present perfect progressive), *he had been writing* (past perfect progressive), and *he will have been writing* (future perfect progressive). Though these are the 12 major tenses, other auxiliary verbs help us show certain conditions (might, may, can), obligations (must), or other meanings (should). Thus: *he can write, he must write,* or *he should have written.*

Adding these auxiliary verbs to show tense or other meanings produces a complex verb. And, as a general rule of style, you should, in order to make your writing clear, avoid gaps between the parts of a complex verb. Naturally, I meant:

> To make your writing clear, you should avoid gaps between the parts of a complex verb.

In the olden days, a popular rule discouraged any words from intruding between the parts of a complex verb. A big No-No: I *have definitely decided* to go to the beach. These days, however, modern stylists recognize the desirability of permitting such small gaps between the auxiliary *have* and the base verb *decided.* Large gaps, however, remain *verboten.*

### Between a verb and its object

Remember that a transitive verb is one that carries an object—a noun following the verb. In a conjugated state, a main verb forms an independent or dependent clause. If that main verb is transitive, its object usually will come somewhere after the verb, unless you're into writing things like *Murder, She Wrote.* In an unconjugated state, a verb forms a verbal phrase, such as an infinitive phrase (*to publish the report*) or a present participial phrase (*publishing the report*). If the verb forming a phrase is transitive, its object must come somewhere after the verb. If you're scratching your head trying to remember all these grammatical terms, you won't scratch much longer. Later in this book, you will learn everything you need to know about verbal phrases. For now, just remember to keep the object of a verb close to the verb. In the negative, do not let a gap disrupt the natural relationship a transitive verb has with its object. Avoid this:

> The Board of Directors has decided *to surrender,* without admitting any responsibility in this matter and with no intent to establish this decision as any kind of precedent for the future, its *rights* under the insurance policy.

The transitive verb *surrender* in its infinitive form *to surrender* yearns for its object *rights*. When you hit your reader with the transitive verb *to surrender*, the reader's mind immediately asks "surrender what?" The faster you answer that question, the tighter your writing will be. Thus, avoid gaps. Keep transitive verbs close to their objects.

### Between the parts of an infinitive: the split infinitive rule

As you might remember, each verb in the English language has an infinitive form. Add the word *to* before any base verb in the language and you get what we think of as the infinitive: *to have, to hold, to love, to honor, to cherish*, to recite part of the wedding vows. As shown above, and as discussed later, these infinitives form phrases, which act as nouns, adjectives, or adverbs. More about that later.

Whenever you use an infinitive, you should try to avoid splitting the *to* from the base verb. Usually, you'll be tempted to put an adverb between the two words, as in *to quickly consider*. Old rules of style would require you to say *quickly to consider* or *to consider quickly*. But inflexible rules of style should not get in the way of clear expression.

Good style, and many stuck-up grammarians, used to forbid splitting infinitives under any circumstances. Good style today, and more realistic grammarians, recognize that rules of style should not get in the way of clarity or grace. If following the no-split-infinitive rule produces an ambiguous statement or grates the ear, you definitely should break the rule in the interest of clarity. You should also ignore the rule in the interest of a graceful style. If the unsplit infinitive is bizarre, go ahead and split. Let's look at an example. Here's my sentence:

We have decided to consider hiring you.

Suppose I want to modify *to consider* with the adverb *quickly*. Following the no-split rule would produce this:

We have decided *quickly to consider* hiring you.

Quickly what? Quickly decided? Or quickly consider? No rule of grammar or style nails my precise meaning. An adverb can come before or after the verb it modifies. Here I've got two verbs: *decided* and *to consider*. Thus, I've produced an ambiguity. Let's try it the other way and still follow the no-split rule:

We have decided *to consider quickly* hiring you.

Again, my reader doesn't have the foggiest idea of my meaning. Am I *quickly considering* or *quickly hiring*? The *only* way to nail my meaning precisely is to split the infinitive as follows:

> We have decided *to quickly consider* hiring you.

Hence the rule: split an infinitive to avoid an ambiguity.

Let's consider some more examples. Fowler provided the following as sentences written by (in his words) "a non-split die-hard." Also, in his words, the sentences are "disasters":

> What alternative can be found which the Pope has not condemned, and which will make it possible *to organize legally* public worship?

> It will, when better understood, tend *firmly to establish* relations between Capital and Labour.

> Both Germany and England have done ill in not combining *to forbid flatly* hostilities.

> Every effort must be made *to increase adequately* professional knowledge and attainments.

> We have had *to shorten somewhat* Lord D's letter.

> The kind of sincerity which enables an author *to move powerfully* the heart would . . . .

> Safeguards should be provided *to prevent effectually* cosmopolitan financiers from manipulating these reserves. (Fowler, pp. 580-81).

Hence another rule: split an infinitive when your ear demands it. After all, what could be worse than going through life as a "non-split die-hard"?

### *Between "that" of a clause and the balance of the clause = the "that-that" problem*

Sometime this week you will hear or see this common mistake. A writer or speaker begins a dependent clause with *that*. He then throws in a gap. He forgets that he already has the *that* setting up the clause.

He throws in another *that*. He ends up with the *that-that* problem. Here's what it looks like:

> This agency has decided *that* regardless of the position taken by your firm in the petition for application for review *that* the petition will be denied.

Remove the gap and read what's left over: This agency has decided *that that* the petition will be denied. Instead, you should keep the *that* close to and part of the clause it introduces:

> Regardless of your firm's position in its petition for review, this agency has decided that the petition will be denied.

What causes these thought-stopping gaps? Usually the writer is breaking the *not-too-many-thoughts-per-sentence rule*. When you find inordinately long sentences in your writing, the chances are good you'll find gaps as well. Look carefully at your main messages and your subordinate messages. You can and should subordinate your subordinate messages. But if those subordinate messages are not truly subordinate or if you are putting too many in one sentence, the inevitable result is gaps.

Set about solving the gap problem and you'll often solve other problems as well. Your reader, for sure, will appreciate the effort.

### Parallel Constructions

Time out for another 10-minute grammar review.

Whenever you say a series of things in a sentence, each part of the series must appear in the same grammatical structure. If the first part of the series is a noun acting as the object of a preposition, each succeeding part must be a noun acting as the object of the same preposition. If the first part of the series is a main verb of a dependent clause, each succeeding part must be a main verb of the same dependent clause. The list of possible parallel constructions, of course, is virtually endless, limited only by the number of grammatical structures in the English language. Perhaps an example will make the rule clear.

You would break the rule if you said: *Yesterday, I went hiking, biking, and took a boat ride.* The first part of the series *hiking* is a present participial verb form; the last part *took* is a conjugated verb form. You would follow the rule if you said: *Yesterday, I went hiking, biking, and boating.*

Where does this rule of parallel construction come from? It is not a rule of style. Rather, it is one of the cardinal rules of grammar. It derives from the definition of *coordinating* and *correlative conjunctions*.

The English language has only three types of conjunctions: *coordinating, correlative*, and *subordinating*. Here we're only concerned with coordinating and correlative conjunctions, but to satisfy your curiosity, let's get subordinating conjunctions out of the way. Subordinating conjunctions join subordinate clauses (or dependent clauses). Subordinating conjunctions are *clause starters*. Samples of subordinating conjunctions include: *when, if, as, because, while, though, although, as long as*, and others. These conjunctions join dependent clauses to independent clauses and play no part in the rule of parallel construction. We'll deal with them at length in a later chapter on the proper use of clauses.

The rule of parallelism instead derives from the coordinating and correlative conjunctions. English has seven coordinating conjunctions: *and, or, but, for, so, yet*, and *nor*. English has only three correlative conjunctions: *not only... but also, neither... nor*, and *either... or*. Each of these joining words must link equal grammatical units. That's what they mean. That's their definition. Hence the rule of parallel construction. The rule comes directly from the meaning of coordinating and correlative conjunctions. To break the rule violates the very definition of these vital words.

Many writers are unfamiliar with the niceties of parallel construction and as a result produce some horrible sentences. For example, today I read the following letter to the editor in the *Washington Post*. Can you spot the nonparallel construction?

> [I]n the defeat they found not only a symbol that rallied them several centuries later to recover their freedom but that served as an inspiration for many literary works and epic poems. (*Washington Post*, A10, October 31, 1988).

Here the writer sought to join two parts of a series with the correlative conjunction *not only... but*. The first part *symbol* serves as the direct object of the transitive verb *found*. Thus, the grammatical structure is established and any additional part of the series joined by the correlative conjunction *must* be a noun acting as the direct object of *found*. But the writer didn't join another noun. Instead, he joined the dependent clause *that served*, which was modifying the word *symbol.*

Two cures come to mind:

> [I]n the defeat they found a symbol that not only rallied them several centuries later to recover their freedom but served as an inspiration for many literary works and epic poems.

> [I]n the defeat they found a symbol not only that rallied them several centuries later to recover their freedom but that served as an inspiration for many literary works and epic poems.

In the first cure, the conjunction joins *rallied* with *served*, two main verbs of the same dependent clause. In the second cure, the conjunction joins *that rallied* with *that served*, two separate dependent clauses. Importantly, the rule of parallelism, one of the cardinal rules of grammar, has been satisfied.

The rule of parallelism, thus, must guide the structure of your sentences. Whenever, in one sentence, you say one thing and then want to say other things, the second and third and fourth things you say must be in the same grammatical construction. That's a fixed, immutable rule of grammar.

You can use the notion of parallel construction in two additional ways as well: (1) you can look at your own writing to see whether you use many parallel constructions at all (the good writers do), and (2) you can search your writing for parallel constructions to determine which structures you favor and which structures you fail to use at all.

We can use the notion of parallel construction to analyze the passage of Mr. Justice Black quoted above. Here it is again. The bracketed numerals precede each parallel construction appearing in the passage:

> Since the earliest days philosophers have dreamed of a country where the mind and [1] spirit of man would be free; [2] where there would be no limits to inquiry; [3] where men would be free to explore the unknown and [4] to challenge the most deeply rooted beliefs and [5] principles. Our First Amendment was a bold effort to adopt this principle — to establish a country with no legal restrictions of any kind upon the subjects people could investigate, [6] discuss and [7] deny. The Framers knew,

better perhaps than we do today, the risks they were taking. They knew that free speech might be the friend of change and [8] revolution. But they also knew that it is always the deadliest enemy of tyranny. With this knowledge they still believed that the ultimate happiness and [9] security of a nation lies in its ability to explore, [10] to change, [11] to grow and ceaselessly [12] to adapt itself to a new knowledge born of inquiry free from any kind of governmental control over the mind and [13] spirit of man. Loyalty comes from love of good government, not [14] fear of a bad one.

To open your eyes, you might take a passage of your own writing, find a paragraph of 180 words or so, and count the number of times you use parallel constructions. Do you have sentences with three main verbs like the one beginning this paragraph? Do you use a variety of parallel constructions as Mr. Justice Black did in the above passage? His structures ranged from three dependent clauses in the first sentence to four consecutive infinitive phrases in the penultimate one.

The notion of parallel construction can also help you analyze habitual structures you favor. Scour your writing for parallel constructions and figure out which structures you tend to repeat in parallel. If you write on a word processor, then have your machine search for the words *and* and *or*. As the cursor lands on each *and* and *or*, look around and identify those structures you are connecting. By looking at those you use, you can identify those you never use. Here's a partial list, along with examples, of some parallel structures that should appear in clear and persuasive writing:

| Structure | Parallel Construction |
|---|---|
| infinitive phrases | To increase the power of your writing, attract the reader's attention, and impress your professor, you should use some infinitive phrases. |
| present participial phrases | Careful writers pay attention to putting their thoughts in phrases and avoiding too many clauses. |
| prepositional phrases | The effective writer argues not only with force but also with style. |
| objects of a prepositional phrase | To write well, pay attention to sentence length, parallel construction, and the rules of tabulation. |

| main verbs in dependent clauses | Though dependent clauses sometimes cloud your messages and confuse your readers, you can use clauses to condense considerable information into one sentence. |
| independent clauses | I came, I saw, I conquered. |

*I came, I saw, I conquered.* See? Even the good writers use parallel constructions. You should too.

### Tabulation

Sometimes the writer is not long-winded. The information is. The main idea of a sentence is qualified in so many ways that a sentence expressing that idea necessarily becomes long and burdensome. In these situations, it is often desirable to present information in a list form. The technique is called tabulation, and nine separate qualifications govern its proper use. In fact, the rules of tabulation are so complex that I figured the best way to present them was by tabulation. Here are the rules of tabulation tabulated.

You can present complicated material in a single sentence by:

1. listing each element of the idea;
2. making each part of the list grammatically and generically the same;
3. indenting the list;
4. numbering the list;
5. introducing the list with a colon;
6. beginning each item on the list with a lowercase letter;
7. ending each item on the list with a semicolon;
8. placing *and* or *or* after the next-to-last item on the list; and
9. ending the list with a period.

Most of these rules are simple and easy to follow. Numbers 2 and 8, however, might cause some trouble. Rule 2 requires the items on the list to be in the same genus or class and to appear in parallel structure. Often, you will find that the rule of parallel construction dictates the genus or class. Some items in your chosen class just will not fit grammatically with the other items on the list. The cure? Change the grammatical construction or narrow the scope of the class.

Rule 8 involves boolean logic. Placing *and* after the penultimate item means that all items on the list are logically necessary. Placing *or* after the penultimate item, however, means that only one item on the list is logically necessary.

### Summary

In this chapter, we have looked at the English sentence from a variety of different angles. We saw how all sentences break down into four broad categories, which are primarily determined by the main verb of the sentence. In those four categories, we saw the three recurring structures of subject, main verb, and the other stuff (adverb, predicate nominative, or predicate adjective). We then studied the vital relationship between sentence length and clarity and saw how, as sentence length goes up, comprehension goes down. We learned to keep sentences short by limiting the number of messages each sentence conveys. We looked at the *subject-predicate = main message rule* and learned to place most of our messages at the subject-verb-object, subject-verb-adverb, subject-verb-adjective, or subject-verb-noun position of the sentence. To give the reader some relief from these structures, we pondered the art of inversion and learned to write backwards. We then ended with techniques of subordination, problems of gaps, the rule of parallel construction, and the device of tabulation.

### The Rules of Good Writing

Your beginning list of the rules of good writing looks like this:

1. Use an average of 25 words per sentence.

2. Avoid putting too many messages in a single sentence.

3. Put most of your messages at the subject-predicate position.

4. For variety or emphasis, invert your sentences.

5. Use the art of subordination to smooth out choppiness.

6. Avoid disrupting your sentences with thought-stopping gaps.

7. Watch out for the rule of parallel construction.

8. Tabulate particularly complex information.

Now let's add to the list by narrowing our focus to a host of habits that prompt professors, bosses, and other powerful people to write this nasty little message in the margins of our papers:

*WORDY!*

Or: *AWKWARD!*

Or worse: *WHAT DO YOU MEAN?*

---

*References*

*Palsgraf v. Long Island Railroad*, 248 N.Y. 339, 162 N.E. 99, 99 (1928).

*Washington Post*, A10, October 31, 1988.

R. Wydick, *Plain English for Lawyers* (1979).

# Chapter 3

# Nouniness — Write with Verbs

*Le mot, c'est le Verbe, c'est Dieu.*

The word is the Verb, and the verb is God.

—Hugo

*A verb has a hard time enough of it in this world when it's all together. It's downright inhuman to split it up. But that's just what those Germans do. They take part of a verb and put it down here, like a stake, and they take the other part of it and put it away over yonder, like another stake, and between these two limits they just shovel in German.*

—Twain

# Chapter 3

## Nouniness — Write with Verbs

### Introduction

This chapter begins our study of the causes and cures of those twin diseases of American, English, Canadian, Australian, and all other expository writing: wordiness and awkwardness. All readers of this book have found this invective glaring at them from the margins of their papers: WORDY! Or perhaps you have found this equally embarrassing tag hanging on your paper: AWKWARD! Is most writing in business, government, and academe wordy? Sure it is. Is it awkward? You betcha. But these are diagnoses. They fail to reveal the root causes of these dread diseases. They certainly suggest no cure.

In this and succeeding chapters, I hope to convince you of the link between grammar and style. I intend to show you a grammatical analysis of wordy writing and to teach you fairly easy grammatical solutions to the problems. When you understand the grammar of *nouniness* (in this chapter) and *clausiness* (in Chapter 6), you'll begin to see some easy ways out of these bad habits. When you learn and begin to use grammatical cures to the problems of wordiness and awkwardness, you will watch needless words disappear before your very eyes. And when you read your finished product and see how it clips along compelling your readers to pay attention, you too will become a believer. You will join the Plain English Movement and vow never again to say:

> While there are instances in which consumer abuse and exploitation result from advertising which is false, misleading, or irrelevant, it does not necessarily follow that these cases need to be remedied by governmental intervention into the marketplace because of the fact that it is possible for consumers' interests to be protected through resort to the courts, either by consumers themselves or by those competing sellers who see their market shares decline in the face of inroads based on such advertising. (*Quoted in* Wydick, pp. 38-39).

Here, in this chapter, we'll tackle the problem of nouniness and learn to write with verbs. Then, in Chapter 6, we'll study the problem of clausiness and learn, ironically, to write with nouns (and other forms). Other chapters will treat a host of other structures that cause us to use too many words to say what we want to say. But first, the big one. Nouniness.

### Grammatical and Typographical Sentences

In writing, there are two kinds of sentences: grammatical and typographical. A grammatical sentence has all the elements we remember from grade school: a subject and a predicate. Grammatical sentences have a subject, a main verb, and, depending on the kind of verb used, a direct object or predicate adjective or predicate nominative or adverb. Typographical sentences, on the other hand, are just a series of words beginning with a capital letter and ending with a period, question mark, or exclamation point. (See Walpole, p. 30.) When writing this and other books, I use typographical sentences all the time. Just look above: *But first, the big one. Nouniness.* Those are two typographical sentences. Though typographical sentences might play some role in formal writing, you primarily will write with grammatical sentences. Typographical sentences in formal writing might come across as too breezy or, worse, as a mistake. They do occur, however. I saw one national columnist begin a paragraph with: *Fat chance.*

To produce a grammatical sentence, you need only one word—a verb. You cannot produce a grammatical sentence with a noun, an adjective, an adverb, or any part of speech other than the verb. The one indispensable word we need is the verb. *Stop. Look. Listen.* Three words. Three verbs. Three grammatical sentences. All else revolves around this crucial word.

Yet for some strange reason, expository writing has all but forsaken the powerful verb. Ironically, writers that pride themselves in their ability to argue persuasively have abandoned the potent verb and chosen in its place the wimpy derivative noun.

### Exhibiting a Preference for Nouns

Instead of *preferring verbs*, many writers exhibit *a preference for* nouns. Don't get me wrong. We can't live, or write, or think without nouns. But there's a special kind of noun that should attract not our favor but our scorn: *the derivative noun.*

A derivative noun derives directly from a base verb. Examples include: *conclusion, preference,* and *statement.* You can spot these derivative nouns by their suffixes: *-ent, -ant, -ence, -ance, -ency, -ancy, -ment* and the all-time favorites *-tion* or *-sion.* Other noun-words have identical verb-words. Examples include: *change, resort,* and *use.*

Suppose a writer wants to express the meaning of the verb *to prefer.* Ordinarily, one would think she would go ahead and use the good old verb *prefer* to say *prefer.* But being a nouny writer, she prefers—whoops, excuse me—she has the preference of using nouns—whoops, pardon me again—she has the preference of noun utilization. There. The nouns won. I mean the nouns experienced a victory.

Undoubtedly, you're getting my drift. Let me continue.

When nouny writers choose the derivative noun to express the meaning of a verb, they face the stark reality of having to write a grammatical sentence. They are left with the dreaded chore of finding a verb on which to hang the noun. They grope around and find the wishy-washiest verbs in these United States of America. And in England. And even in Canada. And probably in Australia. That's right, they find and use the *groped-for verbs.*

### Groped-for Verbs and Other Bits of Noun Glue

Think for a minute.

Finished?

Good. Now back to the book.

It's probably been a few years since you thought for a minute about nouns. But let me guide you through the process. It'll do you a world of good.

There are only two major ways to attach nouns to sentences: (1) with verbs and (2) with prepositions. (Another way, the appositive, will come up later.) Nouns relate directly to verbs as subjects, direct objects, predicate nominatives, objects in verbal phrases, or indirect objects. If you find a noun in a sentence and don't find a verb to which it relates directly, then you'll probably find the second bit of noun glue, the preposition. Indeed, that is what a preposition does. That is the definition of a preposition: *a preposition links a noun to a sentence and shows the relationship of that noun to the rest of the sentence.*

To show you that nouns attach to sentences by sticking to verbs or prepositions, here's an explanation of the noun functions in the sentence you just finished reading:

> That is the *definition* [predicate nominative after the verb *is*] of a *preposition* [object of the preposition *of*]: a *preposition* [subject of the verb *links*] links a *noun* [direct object of the verb *links*] to a *sentence* [object of the preposition *to*] and shows the *relationship* [direct object of the verb *shows*] of that *noun* [object of the preposition *of*] to the *rest* [object of the preposition *to*] of the *sentence* [object of the preposition *of*].

The nouny writers must find verbs or prepositions as hooks for the nouns they use. The verbs they find are the groped-for verbs. Often, the prepositions they find are mushy *compound prepositions*, the topic of a later chapter.

As I stated above, groped-for verbs don't do much for us. They carry very little information. All they do is sit there and hold up nouny constructions. Ironically, these nouny constructions are trying awfully hard to express the meaning of verbs. Here's a partial list of wishy-washy, groped-for verbs along with illustrations of the harm they do:

### The Wishy-Washy, Groped-for Verbs

| Groped-for Verb | Example of Nouniness |
| --- | --- |
| has (and make) | The Freedom of Information Act has pertinence to our agency's duty to make a complete disclosure of information.<br><br>*Translation*: The Freedom of Information Act governs our agency's duty to completely disclose personnel information. |
| take | The Board will take these matters under serious consideration.<br><br>*Translation*: The Board will seriously consider these matters. |
| drew (and reach) | The Board of Directors drew an inference with respect to the applicability of the statute in reaching its decision on this matter.<br><br>*Translation*: When deciding this matter, the Board of Directors inferred that the statute applied. |

| | |
|---|---|
| reached (and was) | The professor reached a conclusion which was favorable to the student's position. |
| | *Translation*: The professor's conclusion favored the student's position. |
| make | The President should make a statement as to the history of this procedure. |
| | *Translation*: The President should describe the history of this procedure. |
| was (and find) | The leader was of the belief that his policies would find vindication in the upcoming economic statistics. |
| | *Translation*: The leader believed that the upcoming economic statistics would vindicate his policies. |

### Derivative Adjectives

A first cousin of the derivative noun is the derivative adjective. Adding the suffixes *-ent, -ant, -ful*, and *-able* often will convert verbs into adjectives. Thus, *hesitant, hopeful*, and *preventable* are adjective substitutes for *hesitate, hope*, and *prevent*. These words have the same effect on your writing as derivative nouns: they are a main cause of wordiness.

### Consequences of Nouniness

The main cause of wordiness is nouniness. If you bury the meaning of verbs in derivative nouns or derivative adjectives, you must come up with other words on which to hang the derivative nouns and derivative adjectives. You must grope around for groped-for verbs to hold up these mushy constructions.

Henry Fowler, in his classic *Modern English Usage*, took aim at the nouny writer and blasted away. If you're a nouny writer, duck:

> Turgid flabby English is full of abstract nouns; the commonest ending of abstract nouns is *-ion*, and to count the *-ion* words in what one has written, or, better, to cultivate an ear that without special orders challenges them as they come, is one of

the simplest and most effective means of making oneself less
unreadable. It is as an unfailing sign of a nouny abstract style
that a cluster of *-ion* words is chiefly to be dreaded. But some
nouny writers are so far from being awake to that aspect of it
that they fall into a still more obvious danger, and so stud their
sentences with *-ions* that the mere sound becomes an offence
.... (Fowler, p. 640).

The sound of it does indeed become an offense. But there is
another drawback to nouniness worthy of even more dread. The nouny
passage is mushy and weak and wimpy. The verb form is powerful and
direct. Noun forms avoid issues. Verb forms hit them head on. Noun
forms lack any sense of motion or action. Verb forms paint vivid pictures
of activity in the reader's mind.

Nothing seems ever to happen in the writing of the nouny writer.
It just sort of sits there, like a couch potato, totally passive and docile.
It always takes matters under consideration. It never considers a thing.
It always places great emphasis upon the fact that .... It never stresses
anything. It always has pertinence to many other things, never once
pertaining to anything at all. It always finds things hesitant. Nothing ever
hesitates.

Because I am dealing with a mature audience, I feel safe in using
my favorite example of nouniness. The noun form wants to avoid issues.
The noun form shies away from telling it like it is. The noun form plays
it safe and shies away. You don't believe me? Then find a socially
acceptable verb describing the sex act. Not out loud, please. The verb
form is much too graphic, clinical, or nasty. Instead of [verb]ing, people
*make love*. Instead of [verb]ing, people *have relations* or *have sex* or
*engage in intercourse*. Never do they [verb]. The closest we've come in
the language to [verbing], I guess, is the verb *do*. But to tone it down,
we follow *do* with the indefinite pronoun *it*.

Obviously, you'll have plenty of occasions to soften your messages,
to avoid issues, to tone it down. The way to do it is with nouns. When
you want to push your opponent gently to the ground, put on your soft
noun gloves. But when you want to hit your opponent with a Mike Tyson
uppercut, bare your fists with verbs.

You must learn the device of (brace yourself) *denounification*.
This well-tested trick will take some of the wimpiest writing around and

make it downright Olympian. To learn the trick, you must first learn the magic of verbs.

### The Five Ways Verbs Work in the English Language

The trick of doing away with nouniness involves converting derivative nouns and derivative adjectives back to verb forms. Before you see the trick in action, you should review the five ways verbs work in the English language. Knowing how verbs act will help you convert derivative nouns and derivative adjectives back into verb forms. When you do convert, you'll produce five different structures.

### *1) The Main Verb*

To show tense or time, verbs are conjugated into one of the six major tenses: *he shows* (present), *he showed* (past), *he will show* (future), *he has shown* (present perfect), *he had shown* (past perfect), and *he will have shown* (future perfect). To show ongoing acts, verbs are conjugated into the progressive tenses, which are formed with the verb *to be* plus the present participle: *he is showing* (present progressive), *he was showing* (past progressive), *he will be showing* (future progressive), *he has been showing* (present perfect progressive), *he had been showing* (past perfect progressive), and *he will have been showing* (future perfect progressive). Other conjugated verbs are formed by using one of the auxiliary verbs plus the base infinitive: *can, must, may, ought, might, shall, should, would, could, be*, and others. Thus: He *must show* the movie.

A main verb forms an independent clause (a sentence) or a dependent clause. Indeed, a clause is defined as *a bunch of words with a main verb in it.* This use, of course, is the primary use of verbs and forms the basic structure of our sentences. The big deal in the English sentence is the conjugated verb—the predicate verb—the *main verb.* Readers know they can expect to find main verbs pinpointing time and serving as the fulcrums of sentences. Indeed, readers search for the main verb in the independent clause fully expecting to find a whole lot of information dwelling there.

The other four verb structures, however, are equally important. These other structures are unconjugated verb forms called *verbals.* They do not pinpoint tense or time but allow us to express the meaning of verbs without setting up the big deal of a clause. Let's look at each in turn.

### 2) The Infinitive Phrase

Every verb has a base, unconjugated form. Identifying the base verb is easy. It's the one you'd look up in the dictionary. We think of the infinitive as the base verb preceded by the word *to*. We use infinitives in our language to form infinitive phrases made up of the infinitive plus other words. Those other words include a noun acting as the object of the infinitive (if the verb is transitive), adverbs modifying the infinitive, and adjectives modifying the noun. Thus: *to win the race decisively*. *To win* is the infinitive, *the race* is the object of the transitive verb *win*, and *decisively* is the adverb modifying the verb form *to win*.

Infinitive phrases can act in three ways—as nouns, adjectives, and adverbs. First, an infinitive can operate as a noun and satisfy many noun functions in the English language. (We'll discuss those functions in Chapter 6.) Here's a direct object: He wanted *to win the race decisively*. Here's a subject: *To win the race decisively* was his goal in life. Second, infinitives can act as adjectives: The man *to beat* is the Democratic candidate for the Senate. Or: The best way *to go* avoids rush-hour traffic. Third, infinitives can act as adverbs: *To win the race decisively,* he trained four hours each day. Or: The homeowner wildly brandished his gun *to scare away the intruder.*

### 3) The Present Participial Phrase

Every verb has a present participle, formed by adding *-ing* to the base verb. As discussed above, present participles do show up in conjugated form in the progressive tenses. But they can also act as unconjugated verbals in participial phrases. The present participial phrase has the present participle of the verb and some other words. Again, if the verb is transitive, the phrase will have a noun acting as the object of that verb. The verb might have adverbs and the noun might have adjectives. All the words collectively form the present participial phrase.

Present participles act as nouns, adjectives, or adverbs. When they act as nouns, they are called *gerunds* and can serve many noun functions. Here's a direct object: He enjoyed *swimming.* Here's a subject: *Winning the race decisively* was his goal in life.

When you use present participial phrases as adjectives, you must be careful about their placement. When a present participial phrase acts as an adjective and begins a sentence, it must modify the subject of the sentence—or the first noun it finds in the independent clause, which is usually the subject. Ever heard of a dangling participle? Here's one: *Marshalling his forces,* the candidacy of Mr. Smith sailed successfully toward election day. Here the present participial phrase *marshalling his forces* needs a subject. The verb *marshalling* seeks an actor, a *marshaller.* The obvious *marshaller* is Mr. Smith. But the first noun encountered in the independent clause is *candidacy.* The participle is unhooked. It just dangles. Revise the sentence and make Mr. Smith the subject: Marshalling his forces, *Mr. Smith* successfully guided his candidacy toward election day.

Other present participial phrases acting as adjectives will *follow* the nouns they modify. In the preceding sentence, the present participial phrase—*acting as adjectives*—followed the noun it modified—*phrases.* Or: The rules *applying to the case before the Honor Council* were passed by the students. (In a later chapter, we'll review the correct punctuation of restrictive and nonrestrictive phrases.)

Also, some very effective present participial phrases come at the tail end of sentences and are usually separated from the rest of the sentence by a comma. Thus: The principal disregarded the evidence, *ruling that it was obtained by an illegal search of the student's locker.*

Finally, present participles can sometimes act as adverbs. The adverbial structure does exist but is rarely encountered. Thus: He died *laughing.*

### 4) The Past Participial Phrase

Every verb also has a past participle. The past participles of regular verbs are formed by adding *-ed.* Thus, the past participle of *exclude* is *excluded.* The past participle of *decide* is *decided.* Other verbs are irregular, having their own unique past participle, usually ending in the letter *n.* Thus, the past participle of *see* is *seen.* The past participle of *show* is *shown.*

Past participles also show up in a conjugated form. With the auxiliary verb *have,* the past participle forms the perfect tenses: *I have shown, I had shown, I will have shown.* Indeed, if you have trouble remembering the past participle of any given verb, simply complete this sentence: *I have* _____. Add the correct verb form. It'll be the past participle of that verb. Also, in a conjugated state, past participles form the passive voice, a topic we'll address in great detail in Chapter 7.

In their unconjugated state, past participles form phrases. These phrases can act only as adjectives and precede or follow the nouns they modify. In a later chapter, we'll see that these participial phrases are the product of discarded passive voice clauses. Thus, don't use a passive voice clause like this: The statute, *which was passed in 1964,* protected our civil rights. Instead, try a past participial phrase like this: The statute, *passed in 1964,* protected our civil rights. Or: *Passed in 1964,* the statute protected our civil rights.

### 5) One-Word Adjectives

The final use of verbs is the one-word participial adjective. These participial adjectives can be present participles or past participles. They are among the most vivid words in the language, describing nouns with verb-like images: *the decided case, the cocked gun, the depreciated property.* All three—*decided, cocked,* and *depreciated*—are past participles. Or: *the winning argument, the limiting factor, the losing team.* All three—*winning, limiting,* and *losing*—are present participles.

How's that for versatility. A verb serves as the pivotal point of the English sentence. The conjugated verb forms that vital fulcrum in our sentence, the independent clause, as well as the dependent clause. The unconjugated verb—the verbal—can function as a noun, as an adjective, and even as an adverb to modify other verbs. The verb does it all. Indeed, one can write a sentence consisting entirely of verbs: *To win is exciting.* No other word in the English language can accomplish as much. In Hugo's words, "The verb is God." Yet many writers have all but abandoned this highly potent word. Instead, they bury the meaning of verbs in piles of nouns like this:

> Amendment of our request is one of our possible courses of action, but if we make a change in our position as of this late date, we might find the official hesitant to place reliance on our exemption arguments. (Adapted from Wydick, p. 80).

There is a much better way.

### Engaging in a Conversion of Nouns to Verbs

Instead of *engaging in a conversion* of nouns to verbs, let's learn *to convert* nouns to verbs. The trick is really quite easy. First, identify derivative nouns, primarily those ending in *-tion, -sion, -ence, -ance, -ency, -ancy,* and *-ment.* Second, be on the lookout for noun-words that can operate as verbs, e.g., *change.* Third, look for nouns you can convert to verbs. *Emphasis,* for example, can convert to *emphasize* or *stress.* (Please, under no circumstances should you change perfectly good nouns like *priority* to perfectly terrible verb forms like *prioritize.* Fowler, no doubt, would go nuclear.)

Once you've identified these mushy noun forms, try converting them to verbs or verbals. Not surprisingly, here's what you'll get: (1) main verbs, (2) infinitive phrases acting as nouns, adjectives, or adverbs, (3) present participial phrases acting primarily as nouns or adjectives, (4) past participial phrases acting as adjectives, and perhaps (5) one-word verb-adjectives.

Let's take the passage above and *engage in a conversion.* Here it is again:

> Amendment of our request is one of our possible courses of action, but if we make a change in our position as of this late date, we might find the official hesitant to place reliance on our exemption arguments.

Here's the same passage after *denounification*:

> We could amend our request, but if we change our position at this late date, the official might hesitate to rely on our exemption arguments.

The first passage has 39 words. The revised passage has 25. Write a 390-page nouny report. I can rewrite the same report in 250 pages. And the only trick I use is *denounification.*

### Piles of Goo—Nouny Expressions of Auxiliary Verbs and Adverbs

Nouns are like rabbits. They breed other nouns. Use one noun structure and it's likely to require other noun structures. Here's why.

Suppose a writer buries the meaning of a verb in a noun form. The writer wishes to say *stop,* but, preferring the longer, fancier-sounding word, uses *termination* instead. Further suppose the writer wishes to say *must stop*. The writer needs the auxiliary verb *must* to say what he wants to say. But by choosing the noun form *termination*, the writer has deprived himself of using some of the most forceful words in the entire language—auxiliary verbs. These wonderful little words pack a real punch in a small amount of space. Think about their crucial meanings: *can, may, must, ought, should, would, might, will,* and others. How, for example, does the nouny writer say *must* (other than *a must*)? Here's one way:

> The effectuation of improvement in our relations with the executive branch has as a requirement our termination of the taking of positions inconsistent with stated executive policy.

The noun *termination*, struggling to convey the meaning of the verb *stop*, bred other nouns when it needed to convey the meaning of the auxiliary verb *must*. Thus: *has as a requirement*.

How does the nouny writer say *can*? Here's a way:

> Amendment of our request is one of our possible courses of action, but if we make a change in our position as of this late date, we might find the official hesitant to place reliance on our exemption arguments.

The noun *amendment*, struggling to say *amend*, multiplied other piles of goo when it wanted to say *could amend*. The noun form required the mushy expression *possible courses of action*.

How does the nouny writer express the crucial meaning of an adverb? Recall that adverbs answer some rather important questions: *where, when, how,* and *why.* If writers bury the meaning of a verb in a noun form, they're in big trouble when they need to modify that idea with an adverb. How does the nouny writer say the adverb *sometimes*? Here's a way:

> There are instances in which consumer abuse and exploitation result from advertising which is false, misleading, or irrelevant.

By using the nouns *abuse* and *exploitation* to bury the meaning of the verbs *abuse* and *exploit*, the nouny writer then buried the meaning of the adverb *sometimes* in the pile of goo *there are instances in which*. Using the verb form, the writer has the true adverb *sometimes* at hand and ready to go:

> Consumers are sometimes abused and exploited by false, misleading, or irrelevant advertising.

Nouns will breed other nouns in other ways as well. As we saw above, we connect nouns to our sentences with verbs or prepositions. In a later chapter, we'll see that a prepositional form favored by the nouny writer is the *compound preposition*, e.g., *in the event of*. Thus, watch what happens when the nouny writer chooses the noun form *use* over the verb form *use*:

> In the event of the employee's use of intoxicating beverages, the employment will terminate.

Converting to verb, of course, changes the wordy compound preposition *in the event of* into a two-letter subordinating conjunction *if*:

> If the employee uses intoxicating beverages, the employment will terminate.

### Write Like Willie Nelson

Though I don't endorse his grammar, I do endorse his style. Willie Nelson, other great writers, and some of the great legal writers of our day all share a secret: they prefer verb forms over noun forms. By using verbs and verbals, they evoke a sense of motion and activity in their writing. With the verb form, they certainly compact information into fewer words—favoring as they do quick, hard-hitting main verbs; succinct, to-the-point infinitives; and tight, action-packed participles. Need proof? Here's Willie singing 39 words. Eighteen of those words are *verb-words*.

> Them that *don't know* him *won't like* him, and them that *do* sometimes *won't know* how *to take* him. He *ain't* wrong, he's just different, and his pride *won't let* him *do* things *to make* you *think* he's right. (*Mama, Don't Let Your Babies Grow Up To Be Cowboys*).

Want to produce an aura of vigor and force? Use verbs. Circuit Judge Frank H. Easterbrook of the United States Court of Appeals in Chicago knows the trick. Listen to his put-down of an attorney who appealed an unappealable order in a case called *Cleaver v. Elias*:

A premature notice of appeal *disrupts* proceedings in the district court. That court *must put* the case aside and *wait* for this one *to send* the record back. Such a notice also *imposes unjustified* costs on the adversary, whose lawyers *must monitor* the case and *file* papers in two courts at once, and on the judges who *must set* things straight. [The attorney] *has filed* such a notice of appeal, after the district judge *told* [him] that there *was* no judgment *to appeal*. *Having sanctioned* [the attorney] under Fed.R.Civ.P. 11 earlier in the case for *filing* an obtuse motion, the district judge *warned* counsel: "I don't think I entered a final judgment order. Now, if you have appealed that, sir, you'll probably get sanctioned up there." [The attorney] *replied*: "I doubt it very much, your Honor." Counsel *should have accepted* this free advice. Our views *are* neither advisory nor free. We *dismiss* the appeal for want of jurisdiction and *impose* a sanction of $1,500 under Fed.R.App.P. 38 *to be paid* by counsel personally.

. . . .

[The attorney] *removed* this case to federal court. It *was* his responsibility *to learn* the fundamentals of federal practice whether the forum *was* of his *choosing* or not. Instead he *filed* and stubbornly *clung* to a silly appeal. Lawyers who *invoke* our jurisdiction without *doing* the necessary groundwork *must expect to pay* for the costs they *impose* on their adversaries and the judicial system. [Citations omitted.] [The attorney's] appeal *caused* the district court *to abort* the hearing on June 13 that *had been called to fix* the amount due on the loan. He *was warned* by the district court and by our order *to show* cause; instead of *dismissing* the appeal he obstinately *pressed forward*. He *is penalized* $1,500 under Rule 38, of which $1,000 *is to be paid* to the plaintiffs as rough compensation for the costs of the *wasted* hearing of June 13 and the need *to monitor* this appeal, and $500 to the Treasury.

Zap! Forty-seven verb constructions. Look at some: *put aside, wait, imposes, monitor, set things straight, caused, pressed forward, doing* and . . . *clung.* If you want to write the same way—powerfully—then the single most important trick in this entire book requires you to use verbs, frequently and effectively.

### Baring Your Knuckles—Using Forgotten Verbs

As I have reviewed many samples of writing, I have come to believe that one of the most vital keys to powerful prose is the effective use of verbs. Inevitably, when reviewing a paper and getting a sense of flab, I can circle main verbs and find lots of *makes, takes, has, is,* and worse *was the result of.* Spotting what's there prompts me to look for what's not there. Looking high and low, inevitably I come up empty in the tally of infinitive phrases, present participial phrases, past participial phrases, and one-word verb-adjectives.

Many writers have forgotten or refused to use the most powerful word in the English language—the verb. In the interest of reviving this lost art form, I urge you to search your memory and find and use hard-hitting verb forms. Try to remember words like *deem, prompt, stress, pinpoint, single out,* and Judge Easterbrook's *cling.* Perhaps we can launch (there's a good one) a campaign to remove the verb from the list of endangered species. Willie and Judge Easterbrook would like that.

### The Rules of Good Writing

Your list of the rules of good writing now looks like this:

1. Use an average of 25 words per sentence.

2. Avoid putting too many messages in a single sentence.

3. Put most of your messages at the subject-predicate position.

4. For variety or emphasis, invert your sentences.

5. Use the art of subordination to smooth out choppiness.

6. Avoid disrupting your sentences with thought-stopping gaps.

7. Watch out for the rule of parallel construction.

8. Tabulate particularly complex information.

9. Hammer home your point with the powerful, versatile verb.

---

*References*

*Cleaver v. Elias,* 852 F.2d 266, 266, 267-68 (7th Cir. 1988).

H. Fowler, *Modern English Usage* (2d ed. 1965).

W. Nelson, *Mama Don't Let Your Babies Grow Up To Be Cowboys.*

J. Walpole, *The Writer's Grammar Guide* (1984).

R. Wydick, *Plain English for Lawyers* (1979).

# Chapter 4

# "To Be" or Not "To Be"

*To be, or not to be: that is the question . . . .*

—Shakespeare

Not "to be": that is the answer.

—Good

# Chapter 4

# "To Be" or Not "To Be"

## Introduction

I learned the answer to this ancient question, as I learn most things about writing, by teaching writing to lawyers. In 1984, I taught a series of persuasive writing courses to attorneys at the Securities & Exchange Commission in Washington and New York. One course, designed for supervising attorneys, stressed the ways to distinguish good writing from bad and methods the supervising attorneys could use to give feedback to the supervised attorneys. During one of these sessions, an attorney brought a sample of a brief she was reviewing. She said, "I know this writing needs help, but I don't know what kind."

I looked at it. And looked. And looked. And looked.

"You're right," I replied. "And I don't know what kind, either."

Then it jumped right off the page at me. I grabbed my pen and began to circle main verbs. The vast majority of the verbs on a single page were various forms of the verb *to be*. The attorney and I agreed that there simply could not be so much *be-ness* running around. The subject matter simply could not involve so much *being*. There just had to be some *doing* somewhere. Some subject matter in the writing had to involve, not *being*, but *happening*. There just had to be some action.

As an experiment, I asked her to return the paper to the writer and instruct him to rewrite the offending page without using the verb *to be* at all, or at least to reduce the number of *be's* on the page. The next week, at the next class session, the attorney showed me the repaired passage. The difference was remarkable. The writing now had flair, vim, and vigor.

Naturally, I hastily repaired to my word processor, called up my course materials, and constructed a giant insert on the verb *to be*. Since that time, I've devoted significant class time to answer the question: *to be* or not *to be*.

My suspicions about the verb *to be* were confirmed when I was teaching a writing workshop to some managers at the Health Care

Financing Administration. One of the class members came to me during
the break following the segment on the verb *to be*. Before working for
the government, he said, he had served as a Jesuit priest, teaching
English at a school in Pittsburgh. He had noticed that high school
students tended to favor the verb *to be* in their speech and their writing.
They, too, had forgotten, or never learned, the potency of action verbs.
To repair the damage, this clever teacher cooked up an assignment
required of all students: write a paper, on any topic, and do not use the
verb *to be* at all. The results, he said, were amazing. The exercise forced
considerable thought and demanded creative use of the language.

### *Like* and *Go*—The Next *Be's*?

Today's high school, college, and even graduate student could
benefit from such an assignment. Today, not only have many students
forgotten the power of verbs, they've invented incredible crutch-words
that pepper their spoken language. Sooner, rather than later, these
words or similar weak expressions will show up in their written language.
These crutch-words come, I think, from Saturday morning cartoons and
"Valley Speak" in California. One day, I hope, they'll leave as quickly
as they came. If they don't, they threaten to diminish our language
significantly.

Though I'm no etymologist, I firmly believe that *like* and *go* came
directly from television. Think about the two primary ways young people
use *go*. First, it serves as a catchall verb substituting for *said, stated,
asked, replied, responded,* or other verb meaning *to speak.* Thus, students
might go:

> My teacher asked the hardest question in class today. She went,
> "How does the Bill of Rights affect the 50 states?"
>
> Did she call on you?
>
> Sure did, and I went, "Don't the states have to provide the same
> rights?"
>
> And she went, "I'm asking you."
>
> So I went, "Yes, they have to provide the same rights."
>
> Next time I'll go like . . . .

The second use of *go* proves its origins in television. Today's elocutionist, when describing an event, might go like:

> He was running long for the pass. He went [speaker extends arms indicating a reaching motion desperately seeking to connect with the spiraling pigskin]. When he jumped, he went [speaker then whistles from a high *C* down the chromatic scale and immediately follows this noise with an explosive, guttural sound-effect roughly equivalent to a Madden-like *whap*.]

The only words used?

> He was running long for the pass. He went.... When he jumped, he went "whap."

One can readily see the connection between television and speech. Just conjure up the image of the typical cartoon character running off the side of a cliff. He continues running in air, realizes the disappearance of ground beneath his feet, panics, begins plummeting wildly to earth to the tune of a whistle down the chromatic scale, and meets his Maker in an ear-splitting collision with Mother Earth—all of which is brought to life by the sound-effect guy in the back room dropping on a concrete slab an overly ripe watermelon from a 10-foot ladder. When asked what happened, the child describes, not what happened, but *what he saw*:

> He went [arms flail wildly in air, whistle down the chromatic scale, terror-stricken expression on face] "whap."

*He went "whap."* That's it. That's the extent of the language. No other thoughts or expressions of thought are possible. Nor allowed. Nor, worse, understood. When I talked about this problem with my own two sons, the elder, tongue firmly in cheek, went, "Dad, I wonder who was the first person who went 'go'?" I don't know who first *went "go"* but if we continue *to go "go"* and convey our meaning with special visual and sound effects, we can forget about verbs forever.

*Go* has mutated into an even worse expression: *was-like*. One day, we'll close this compound and have a new word *waslike* or *islike* or even *wasgoinglike*. Listen to the speech around you:

> He waslike, "I just couldn't get out of bed this morning."

> Did he like have a bad night?

> Like, he waslike uhhhhh. He had a six-pack in like an hour.

Do *golikers* really threaten our language? You'd better believe they do. The national press even provides direct quotations of this scourge. While I was putting the finishing touches on this book in the fall of 1988, the valiant Eskimos, marine biologists, and Russian sailors were trying to save the two ice-bound whales off Barrow, Alaska. Quoting the rescue coordinator, the *Washington Post* put the following in one of those boxes designed to catch the reader's attention. It certainly caught mine.

> These guys [the Russians] were all business. We got on board
> and they were like, "Let's go break ice." [*Washington Post* at A3
> (October 26, 1988)].

The Valley Girls and their bubble gum have like messed up our like language. Spit it out, folks, or your writing will suffer as well. The *go-like* talk will probably show up in writing in the form of too many *be's*. "To be or not to be, that is the question." Not *to be*. Not *go*. Not *like*. Not *waslike*. Those are the answers.

### The Meaning of the Verb *To Be*

Before studying the proper use of the verb *to be*, we would do well to explore its meaning and use in the English language. When used as the main verb of a sentence or clause, the verb *to be* shows a state of being, the existence of something, or a condition. The verb follows a subject and shows the existence of that subject or some condition of that subject. These meanings become plainer when you contemplate grammatical constructions of the verb *to be*.

Rarely, but sometimes, the verb *to be* can appear by itself. Ask Neal Diamond. "I am, I said," he sang. Most of the time, the verb *to be* will be followed by a noun (predicate nominative) or an adjective (predicate adjective). And in some cases, the verb *to be* can be followed by an adverb. Let's look at each construction to see what it means.

When the verb *to be* is followed by a noun (predicate nominative or subject complement), that noun restates or defines the subject of the sentence. Thus: *The development of the PC was a landmark in the history of the computer industry*. Development was landmark. The predicate nominative *landmark* defines *development*; it tells what the development *was*.

When the verb *to be* is followed by an adjective (predicate adjective), that adjective describes the subject of the sentence. This structure is one of the few ways in the English language to get an adjective to follow the word it modifies. Thus: *The decision of the agency was instrumental in increasing competition in the telecommunications industry.* Decision was instrumental. The predicate adjective *instrumental* describes *decision*; it states the condition of the decision.

The verb *to be* might be followed by a prepositional phrase. Thus: *He was from the north.* Or: *He was for Bush.* Or: *He is like a child.*

In some situations, the verb *to be* might be followed by an adverb. Recall that adverbs answer four questions: *when, where, how,* and *why.* Though adverbs cannot say *how* or *why* someone *is*, they can say *where* or *when* someone *is.* Thus: *He is here.* Or: *He is late.* But not: *He is "quickly."*

Finally, I should point out that *to be* also acts as an auxiliary verb. Coupled with a present participle, it forms the progressive tenses:

he is showing

he was showing

he will be showing

he has been showing

he had been showing

he will have been showing

Also, when used with a past participle the verb *to be* forms the passive voice of that verb:

the movie is shown

the movie was shown

the movie will be shown

the movie has been shown

the movie had been shown

the movie will have been shown

We will return to the passive voice for extensive discussion in a later chapter. For now we are interested in *to be* not as an auxiliary, but as the main verb of an independent or dependent clause.

### The Rule: Use the Verb *To Be* Only When You Mean It

The verb *to be* properly defines or describes. When you truly want to say what something *is* or what something *is like*, use the verb *to be*. However, if you want to say what something *does*, but use the verb *to be* as a means of showing *doing*, you will end up with inordinately flabby writing.

Not surprisingly, writers that overuse the verb *to be* tend to be nouny writers as well. Recall that the verb *to be* is an ideal *groped-for* verb on which to hang derivative nouns and derivative adjectives. Thus, watch out for this:

> The board was of the belief that a precondition of an increase in income was an increase in national advertising.

Getting rid of *be's* and engaging in denounification produce this:

> The board believed that increasing national advertising would increase income.

As another example, check out the abundance of *be's* in this passage, which is describing the nature of a Senate resolution confirming a President's judicial nominee:

> This definition leads us to conclude that the nature of a resolution is that it is a formal expression of opinion that has only a temporary effect or no effect at all as a legal matter. The Senate's confirmation vote is an expression of the opinion of the Senate as to whether the Senate will advise and consent to the nomination. This expression of opinion by formal vote is, in substance, virtually identical to the meaning of a resolution. However, it is not clear that the Senate's confirmation vote merely expresses an opinion and has only a temporary effect on a particular matter or thing. While the advice and consent offered by the Senate is an expression of opinion, it is not merely an expression of opinion because it has consequences that ordinarily do not result from the mere expression of an opinion. In short, although the Senate itself labels its confirmation vote a resolution, that vote is in substance not a resolution, but is placed somewhere in the spectrum between Acts and bills, on the one side, and resolutions, on the other side.

Now look at the same passage written without any *be's* instead of the nine used above:

This definition helps us understand the nature of a resolution. A resolution formally expresses the Senate's opinion and has only a temporary effect or no effect at all as a legal matter. The Senate's confirmation vote also expresses the Senate's opinion on whether it will advise and consent to the nomination. Expressing this opinion by formal confirmation vote closely resembles a Senate resolution. However, the Senate's confirmation vote does more than merely express an opinion. It has a lasting, not a temporary, effect on a particular matter or thing. While the advice and consent of the Senate in the confirmation vote does express its opinion, the vote has consequences that go beyond the mere expression of an opinion. In short, although the Senate itself labels its confirmation vote a resolution, that vote differs from a resolution. The vote falls somewhere between Acts and bills, on the one side, and resolutions, on the other side.

As a final example, let's look at Henry Steele Commager's writing in *The American Mind* and see how he uses the verb *to be* when he means it and avoids it when he doesn't:

The American's attitude toward authority, rules and regulations was the despair of bureaucrats and disciplinarians. Nowhere did he differ more sharply from his English cousins than in his attitude toward rules, for where the Englishman regarded the observance of a rule as a positive pleasure, to the American a rule was at once an affront and a challenge. His schools were almost without discipline, yet they were not on the whole disorderly, and the young girls and spinsters who taught them were rarely embarrassed. This absence of discipline in the schools reflected absence of discipline in the home. Parents were notoriously indulgent of their children and children notoriously disrespectful of parents, yet family life was on the whole happy, and most children grew up to be good parents and good citizens.

Notice, in describing what a rule *was* and how the teachers *were* and how the schools *were*, Mr. Commager appropriately used the verb *to be*. But also notice his sentence:

This absence of discipline in the schools reflected absence of discipline in the home.

Notice what he didn't say:

> This absence of discipline in the schools *was the result of* absence of discipline in the home.

Good writers use *to be* only when they mean it.

### Expletive Deleted

Before moving on to another first cousin of nouniness—compound prepositions—we should glance quickly at a special construction of the verb *to be*, the expletive. These expletives are not the notorious "expletives deleted" of Watergate-tape-transcript fame. Those expletives were President Nixon's gutter language.

The expletive we discuss here is a surrogate noun expression like *there are, these are, it is,* and *this is*. In these expressions (called expletives), *there, these, it,* or *this* serves as a substitute noun for the true subject of the sentence. Look at the following sentence:

> There are numerous cases of child abuse in the state of Massachusetts.

The grammatical subject is *there*. The verb is *are*. The grammatical predicate nominative is *cases*. The true subject of the sentence, however, is *cases*. The word *there* just stands in the place of *cases*.

Ordinarily, there is nothing wrong with this structure. I just used it. *There is nothing wrong with this structure.* However, if the expletive is followed by a *that* or *which* clause, and if you use lots of these expressions, chances are good your sentences beg for revision. Here are some examples:

> It was the belief of the board that the employee's delay would be a bar to recovery.

> There are several factors that the agency must take into consideration when it decides on the violation of the rule.

> This is one important factor that all teachers place great emphasis upon.

No, no, no. When you spot this kind of writing, delete the expletive and make the true subject of the sentence the grammatical subject as well:

> The board believed that the employee's delay would bar recovery.

> The agency must consider several factors when it decides if the rule has been violated.

> All teachers emphasize this one important factor.

## Summary

In this chapter, we've looked carefully, and somewhat harshly, at the verb *to be*. My harsh look is not meant to suggest the abolition of the verb. Indeed, by definition, we just could not be without it.

What I suggest is careful thought. When you truly want to show *being*, use *to be*. But whenever you can, choose a vigorous action verb to carry your thought. Without any doubt, the powerful writer uses heavy doses of verbs other than the verb *to be*. Give it a try. Your writing will be better. I mean, your writing will improve.

## The Rules of Good Writing

Your list of the rules of good writing now looks like this:

1. Use an average of 25 words per sentence.
2. Avoid putting too many messages in a single sentence.
3. Put most of your messages at the subject-predicate position.
4. For variety or emphasis, invert your sentences.
5. Use the art of subordination to smooth out choppiness.
6. Avoid disrupting your sentences with thought-stopping gaps.
7. Watch out for the rule of parallel construction.
8. Tabulate particularly complex information.
9. Hammer home your point with the powerful, versatile verb.
10. Use the verb *to be* only when you mean it.

---

*Reference*

*Washington Post*, A3, October 26, 1988.

# Chapter 5

# Compound Prepositions —
# The Compost of our Language

*[He] is as brisk as a bee in conversation; but no sooner does he take a pen in his hand, than it . . . benumbs all his faculties.*

—Samuel Johnson

# Chapter 5

# Compound Prepositions—

# The Compost of our Language

## Introduction

Lots of writers love *with respect to, in reference to, in connection with, for the purposes of,* and similar expressions. In this chapter, I hope to convince you to avoid these *compound prepositions* altogether. If you're hooked, however, perhaps I can get you to reduce your use of these expressions in the interest of vastly improving your writing.

This chapter first will define the preposition, the prepositional phrase, and the compound preposition. Our discussion will then provide an all-out scathing attack on the compound preposition by one of the great stylists of our time. Then you'll find examples of the compound-preposition style and see just how vague these expressions are. At the end, I'll provide a list of compound prepositions and their simpler substitutes.

## Preposition and Prepositional Phrase Defined

In the chapter on nouniness, you learned that nouns must be glued to sentences by verbs or prepositions. If glued by verbs, nouns serve as subjects or objects of main verbs or verbals. The other major way to glue nouns onto sentences is by the preposition. Looked at in this way—as one of the primary noun-attachers—the preposition readily finds its own definition:

> A preposition is a word used to link a noun or noun form to a sentence and to show the relationship the noun bears to another noun or to a verb.

From the definition of a preposition, we can glean the definition of a prepositional phrase:

> A prepositional phrase consists of a preposition and a noun or noun form acting as the object of the preposition.

A preposition links a noun or noun form to a sentence. Coupled with that noun or noun form, it produces a prepositional phrase. Note that the preposition links a noun and shows the relationship of that noun to another noun in the sentence or to a verb in the sentence. Thus, the prepositional phrase primarily serves two roles in the English sentence. First, by showing the relationship of a noun to another noun, the prepositional phrase acts as an *adjective*. For example: The man *in the front row* paid a hefty price *for his ticket*. The prepositional phrase *in the front row* modifies the noun *man*. And the prepositional phrase *for his ticket* modifies the noun *price*. Thus, the prepositional phrase serves its first function, that of an adjective. Second, by showing the relationship of a noun to a verb, the prepositional phrase acts as an *adverb*. For example: He ran *down the street* to see the approaching parade. The prepositional phrase *down the street* modifies the verb *ran* by telling *where* he ran. (Please note in the example that *to see the approaching parade* is an infinitive phrase, not a prepositional phrase.) The prepositional phrase thus serves its second function, that of an adverb. (I should note that a prepositional phrase might act as a noun: *After six* is a good time to call.)

A preposition connects a noun to a sentence and, with that noun, forms a phrase acting primarily as an adjective or adverb. The key is the noun—the object of the preposition. Without that noun, the preposition cannot even be in a sentence. At least it cannot serve as a preposition. Without the noun, a word that otherwise would be a preposition must act in some other way.

Take the word *down* as an example. If used in a sentence in some way other than to link a noun to the sentence, the word cannot be a preposition. Consider this sentence: He looked *down the hill* to see the sporting event. Here *down* is used as a preposition in the adverbial prepositional phrase *down the hill* to modify *looked*. Now try this: He looked *down* to hunt for coins. The sentence is almost identical. But the word *down* lacks a noun to link to the rest of the sentence. Therefore, the word *down* is not and cannot be a preposition. It functions as a simple adverb modifying *looked*.

Notice in the above definitions that a noun or *noun form* must join with a preposition to form a prepositional phrase. These *noun forms* include present participles and noun clauses. We've already dealt with present participles acting as nouns. When they do, they're called *gerunds.* Here's one acting as the object of a preposition: He became adept in *coaching his players.* In that sentence, the present participial phrase *coaching his players* acts as the object of the preposition *in.*

The other noun form that can serve as the object of a preposition is the *noun clause.* We will deal extensively with noun clauses in a later chapter. Here, I'll only provide an example of a noun clause used as the object of a preposition and postpone any analysis of noun clauses and the damage they often do to our language:

> Your supervisor was aware of *the fact that you bought this book.*

The noun clause *the fact that you bought this book* serves as the object of the preposition *of.*

### The Importance of Prepositions

Why does a book on expository writing include a discussion of prepositions? For this very good reason: many writers not only have abandoned the hard-hitting verb but have lost touch with the simple, but forceful, preposition. Indeed, many writers might have asked the above question this way: "Why does a book with regard to expository writing include a discussion with respect to prepositions?"

Many writers ignore simple, powerful prepositions like *on* and *of.* They prefer instead fluffy prepositions like *with regard to* and *with respect to.* Learning to discard these *compound prepositions* requires an understanding of the grammatical role of prepositions. That's why this book contains a discussion with respect to prepositions.

### Compound Preposition Defined

A *compound preposition* is a series of prepositional phrases that combine to act as a single preposition. Examples include:

> with respect to
> with regard to
> in connection with
> for the purposes of

The beginning of a compound preposition is an apparently complete prepositional phrase. In the above examples, note these apparently complete prepositional phrases:

> with respect
> with regard

in connection
for the purposes

Yet these apparently complete prepositional phrases could not function in sentences alone. They need to combine forces with another preposition so that together they can link a noun to a sentence.

*with respect to* your <u>request</u>
*with regard to* your <u>request</u> for a raise
*in connection with* the <u>sale</u> of securities
*for the purposes of* <u>determining</u> total tax owed

In the above list, the italicized compound prepositions serve to link the underlined nouns. The compound preposition needs the apparently complete prepositional phrase *with respect* and the additional preposition *to* to form a single expression acting as a single preposition—*with respect to.*

That's what compound prepositions are. That's what compound prepositions do. That's what compound prepositions look like. Now let's go after them with a vengeance.

**Garbage**

I hope that heading attracts attention. I didn't make it up. The thought belongs to Henry Fowler. Here's what he has to say about compound prepositions:

> [T]aken as a whole, they are almost the worst element in modern English, stuffing up what is written with a compost of nouny abstractions. To young writers the discovery of these forms of speech, which are used very little in talk and very much in print, brings an expansive sense of increased power; they think they have acquired with far less trouble than they expected the trick of dressing up what they may have to say in the right costume for public exhibition. Later they know better, and realize that it is feebleness instead of power that they have been developing; but by that time the fatal ease that the compound-preposition style gives (to the writer, that is) has become too dear to be sacrificed. (Fowler, p. 102).

If you are hooked on compound prepositions, you will dramatically improve your writing by sacrificing the compound-preposition style. They clutter up our language and fail to convey our precise meaning.

Nouny writers necessarily favor the compound-preposition style, needing as they do lots of prepositions on which to hook their nouns. Thus, the nouny writer is likely to say:

> In the event of the employee's use of intoxicating beverages, the employment will terminate.

Obliterating the noun *use* and changing it to the verb *uses* also erases the need for the compound preposition. Its meaning shifts to the subordinating conjunction *if*:

> If the employee uses intoxicating beverages on the job, the employment will terminate.

### Imprecision

Compound prepositions do more than clutter. They prevent or at least hinder precision in our writing. These expressions often are so imprecise that they should be abolished from our language. Consider one of the all-time favorites, *with respect to*. In the following passage, watch what happens to its meaning:

> The problem *with respect to* the compound preposition is its ability to experience a shift *with respect to* meaning. *With respect to* some sentences, it can mean one thing, while *with respect to* other sentences it might have something else to say *with respect to* some other topic.

Need a translation? Watch the meaning of *with respect to* shift from one preposition to an entirely different one.

> *Translation*: The problem *with* the compound preposition is its ability to experience a shift *in* meaning. *In* some sentences, it can mean one thing, while *in* other sentences it might have something else to say *about* some other topic.

Next, think about the expression *for the purposes of* plus an *-ing* verb, a gerund. You can and should convert all these prepositional phrases to infinitive phrases using the infinitive of the *-ing* verb. For example:

| | |
|---|---|
| for the purposes of ascertaining intent | to ascertain intent |
| for the purposes of determining income | to determine income |
| for the purposes of inspecting the property | to inspect the property |

Try declaring war on compound prepositions. At first the change will sound strange. Once you get used to it, however, you'll definitely prefer the clearer, more direct style.

### A List of Compound Prepositions

To assist you in converting compound prepositions to simpler prepositions or to other grammatical forms, here's a partial list showing compound prepositions and the simpler expressions that should replace them:

| Compound Preposition | Simple Expression |
|---|---|
| at that point in time | then |
| at this point in time | now |
| by means of | by |
| by reason of | because of |
| by virtue of | by, under |
| during the course of | during |
| for the purposes of [+ noun] | for, under |
| for the purposes of [+ gerund] | infinitive phrase |
| from the point of view of | from, for |
| in accordance with | by, under |
| in a manner similar to | like |
| in excess of | more than, over |
| in favor of | for |
| in receipt of | having received |
| in relation to | about, concerning |
| in terms of | in |
| in the nature of | like |
| in the immediate vicinity of | near |
| in close proximity with | near |
| on the basis of | by, from |
| with a view to | to |
| with reference to | about, concerning |
| with regard to | about, concerning |
| with respect to | on, about, for, in, concerning, with, to |

## Some Common Prepositions You Might Have Forgotten

aboard

about

above

according to

across

after

against

along

alongside of (or alongside)

along with

amid or amidst

among or amongst

apart from

around

as against

as between

as for

aside from

as to

at

barring

because of

before

behind

below

beneath

beside

besides

between

beyond

by

concerning

considering

despite

down

during

excepting (or except)

exclusive of

for

from above

from among

from behind

from beneath

from between

from over

from under

in

including

inclusive of

independently of

in front of

in lieu of

inside of (or inside)

in spite of

instead of

into

like

notwithstanding

of

off

on

on account of

on behalf of

onto

opposite to (or opposite)

out of

outside of (or outside)

over

owing to

past

pending
regarding
regardless of
relating to
relative to
respecting
round
saving
short of
since
through
throughout
to

touching
toward (or towards)
under
underneath
until (or till)
unto
up
upon
via
with
within
without

## The Rules of Good Writing

Your list of the rules of good writing now looks like this:

1. Use an average of 25 words per sentence.
2. Avoid putting too many messages in a single sentence.
3. Put most of your messages at the subject-predicate position.
4. For variety or emphasis, invert your sentences.
5. Use the art of subordination to smooth out choppiness.
6. Avoid disrupting your sentences with thought-stopping gaps.
7. Watch out for the rule of parallel construction.
8. Tabulate particularly complex information.
9. Hammer home your point with the powerful, versatile verb.
10. Use the verb *to be* only when you mean it.
11. Get rid of compound prepositions.

---

*Reference*

H. Fowler, *Modern English Usage* (2d ed. 1965).

# Chapter 6

# Clausiness — Write with Nouns (And Phrases)

*. . . let thy words be few.*

—Ecclesiastes 5:2

# Chapter 6

## Clausiness — Write with Nouns

## (And Phrases)

### Introduction

In Chapter 3, you learned to remember the forgotten verb. Nouniness, you discovered, is one of the main features of a stuffy style. Converting derivative nouns and derivative adjectives to base verbs, infinitive phrases, present participial phrases, past participial phrases, or one-word verb-adjectives always tightens up your writing and produces a more powerful style. The verb, you learned, is one of the more versatile words in the English language. It can act as verb, noun, adjective, or adverb. No other word, in fact, can serve all these grammatical needs as easily as the verb. We learned in Chapter 3, therefore, to prefer verbs. We learned to forego *groped-for* verbs and place our messages in straightforward verbs and verbal phrases. We learned, in short, a basic truth about our language: *When a sentence goes begging for a verb, give it a verb.*

Now let's learn the opposite. Let's learn to avoid too many verb structures. Let's learn all about clauses. Let's learn that a clause is a *big deal*, which, when sparingly used, drives home our arguments. Let's learn that too many *big deals* diminish our points. Let's learn to cut clauses and write with nouns, adjectives and adverbs, prepositional phrases, verbal phrases, and other structures called appositives. Write with nouns? Am I kidding? No I'm not. Am I preaching two contradictory messages? Again, no I'm not. In this chapter, you'll learn another basic truth about our language: *When a sentence goes begging for a noun, give it a noun.*

Simple. When a sentence wants a verb, give it a verb, not a noun. When a sentence wants a noun, give it a noun, not a verb. Seems clear to me. Let me make it clear to you.

## Clauses Defined

Recall our discussion of verbs. To show when something takes place, we conjugate verbs to indicate time or tense. The six major tenses include present, past, future, present perfect, past perfect, and future perfect. We can show only two—present and past—with one *verb-word.* Thus: *I write* (present) and *I wrote* (past). All the others require *helping verbs*, also called *auxiliary verbs.* Thus: *I will write* (future), *I have written* (present perfect), *I had written* (past perfect), and *I will have written* (future perfect).

Other major tenses include the progressive tenses, formed by conjugating the verb *to be* and adding the present participle. Thus: *I am writing* (present progressive), *I was writing* (past progressive), *I will be writing* (future progressive), *I have been writing* (present perfect progressive), *I had been writing* (past perfect progressive), and *I will have been writing* (future perfect progressive).

With these twelve tenses, you can mix all sorts of auxiliary verbs to achieve any meaning you need: *I might have been writing. He should have written. The agency could have written the report.*

Using any of these main verb forms will create a clause. Hence the definition of a clause:

A clause is a bunch of words with a main verb in it.

Clauses break down into two large categories: independent and dependent. An independent clause is simply a complete sentence. It needs nothing else to express a complete thought that has all the elements of an English sentence. Here are two independent clauses:

The board could have raised prices.

I should have been writing.

A dependent clause, on the other hand, also has a main verb but cannot stand by itself as a complete sentence. To form a sentence, it must connect to an independent clause. Here are two dependent clauses:

Though the board could have raised prices

although I should have been writing

Neither of those two statements qualifies as an independent clause. They are not complete sentences. Our English teachers of yore would have screamed: "Fragments!"

### Clause Starters

#### *Subordinating Conjunctions*

To form complete sentences, these dependent clauses must be joined to independent clauses. One word that does the "joining" and makes certain clauses dependent is the *subordinating conjunction.* We previously discussed the three kinds of conjunctions in the English language—the *coordinating conjunction,* the *correlative conjunction,* and the *subordinating conjunction.* The first two—*coordinating* and *correlative*—are used to join equal grammatical units (remember the rule of parallel construction?) and to join independent clauses. The last—the *subordinating conjunction*—joins a dependent clause to an independent clause.

Below we'll discuss the three functions of dependent clauses and learn that they may serve as nouns, adjectives, or adverbs. The subordinating conjunction typically introduces an adverb clause—one that modifies the verb of the independent clause. Remember that adverbs answer these four questions: *where, when, how,* and *why.*

Thus, here's a dependent adverb clause modifying the verb of the independent clause. Notice that the clause tells *why* the board *decided* to raise prices:

> Because the cost of paper had increased dramatically, the board decided to raise prices.

Here's a list of the most frequently used subordinating conjunctions. As you review the list, think about the adverbial questions such clauses would answer about the verbs they modify. For example, *because* answers the question *why. As* answers the question *when* or *why.*

<u>Subordinating Conjunctions</u>

| | |
|---|---|
| after | because |
| although | before |
| as | even though |
| as long as | if |
| as soon as | insofar as |
| as well as | like |

since                              whereas
though                             whether
when                               while
where

Please notice that some of these subordinating conjunctions can serve dual roles. Some can act not only as a conjunction but also as a preposition. For example, here are some samples of these words used as subordinating conjunctions and as prepositions:

| Subordinating Conjunction | Preposition |
|---|---|
| He warmed up *before* he lifted weights. | He warmed up *before* exercise. |
| He was still hungry *after* he ate lunch. | He was still hungry *after* lunch. |
| He hasn't played *since* he was injured. | He hasn't played *since* his injury. |

Although subordinating conjunctions do begin adverb clauses, I don't want to leave you with the notion that those are the only clauses they introduce. They can also start adjective clauses: I walked on the street *where you live.*

### Relative Pronouns

Subordinating conjunctions are not the only *clause starters.* Adjective clauses are joined to independent clauses by *relative pronouns.* Here are the most common:

Relative Pronouns

that                whom
which               whose
who

Here are two adjective clauses. Each modifies the noun *division.*

The top division, *which earned more income than any other division in the company,* rewarded its personnel with cash incentives.

We know all about the division *that failed.*

Most people routinely confuse the relative pronouns *that* and *which*. For that reason, I've discussed below the differences between these relative pronouns and the crucial differences between restrictive and nonrestrictive clauses.

### Other Clause Starters

The final *clause starters* are those that begin noun clauses, clauses acting as nouns. These words don't really have a name like *subordinating conjunction* or *relative pronoun*. Instead, each might serve a different function within the clause itself. For example: We'll never know *how he writes so many books*. Here the noun clause *how he writes so many books* acts as the direct object of the transitive verb *know*. The word *how* starts the noun clause. It serves as an adverb within the clause, modifying the verb *writes*. Whatever their names, here's a partial list of these *noun clause starters*:

Noun Clause Starters

| | |
|---|---|
| that | why |
| the fact that | where |
| what | whether |
| how | whoever |

Here's a typical noun clause, one that might show up in expository writing:

> The agency was aware of the fact that many of its top people were leaving.

The clause—*the fact that many of its top people were leaving*—acts as a noun. It serves as the object of the preposition *of*.

Those are the three *clause starters*: the *subordinating conjunctions* (primarily for adverb clauses), the *relative pronouns* (for adjective clauses), and *a special group of clause starters* (for noun clauses).

Let's first study the three kinds of dependent clauses: noun clauses, adjective clauses, and adverb clauses. We'll learn how crucial these clauses are to our language. Then, however, we'll see that expository writers usually rely too heavily on the clause to express their thoughts. Hence, we'll conclude with a review of the ways you can successfully cut clauses down to nouns, prepositional phrases, adjectives and adverbs, verbal phrases, and appositives. And when you cut a clause, what do you get rid of? Those wonderful words we learned to love in Chapter 3: the main verbs.

### Three Kinds of Clauses

Dependent clauses serve three roles in the English language. They can act as nouns, adjectives, or adverbs. If they act as nouns, they're called *noun clauses*. If they act as adjectives, they're called *adjective clauses*. Finally, if they act as adverbs, they're called *adverb clauses*. Because we are moving toward a rule favoring the cutting of clauses, you must first understand the nature and function of all three.

### *The Noun Clause*

The noun clause is *a bunch of words with a main verb in it* that acts just as any noun would act in the English language. So that you can see how noun clauses act in English, when you use them, and when you cut them out, a 10-minute review of grammar is in order—a review of the role of nouns.

Recall your English teacher's definition? A noun is a person, place, thing, or idea. Good definition. It covers the bases. Do you remember all eight functions of the noun in the English language? If not, you should know them and know them cold. Here they are with italicized examples of each.

| Eight Noun Functions | Italicized Example |
| --- | --- |
| 1. Subject | Overruling the supervisor, the *vice-president* of the department, William Womble, gave the issue his immediate attention. |
| 2. Direct Object | Overruling the supervisor, the vice-president of the department, William Womble, gave the issue his immediate *attention*. |
| 3. Indirect Object | Overruling the supervisor, the vice-president of the department, William Womble, gave the *issue* his immediate attention. |

| | |
|---|---|
| 4. Object of a Preposition | Overruling the supervisor, the vice-president of the *department*, William Womble, gave the issue his immediate attention |
| 5. Object in a Verbal Phrase | Overruling the *supervisor*, the vice-president of the department, William Womble, gave the issue his immediate attention. |
| 6. Appositive | Overruling the supervisor, the vice-president of the department, *William Womble*, gave the issue his immediate attention. |
| 7. Subject Complement (Predicate Nominative) | He will be the next corporate *president*. |
| 8. Object Complement | We elected him *president*. |

In the above sentences, I used true nouns or proper nouns to serve the eight noun functions. We've already seen how unconjugated verbals (infinitives and present participles) can satisfy noun functions. Now let's see how main verbs can do the same thing.

A noun clause—*a bunch of words with a main verb in it*—can serve all eight noun functions. As my example, I'll choose a *the fact that* clause, one of the worse constructions in the English language. I'm not alone. My opinion is shared by Mr. Strunk and Mr. White. Here's what they have to say:

> An expression that is especially debilitating is *the fact that*. It should be revised out of every sentence in which it occurs. (Strunk & White, p. 24).

Right now let's see how a *the fact that* noun clause works. Later we'll see exactly how to revise it out of every sentence in which it occurs. Here's my noun clause: *the fact that you came to this course*. Here's the same clause serving all eight noun functions.

| Eight Noun Functions | Italicized Example |
|---|---|
| 1. Subject | *The fact that you came to this course* shows your interest in clear writing. |
| 2. Direct Object | Your boss applauded *the fact that you came to this course.* |
| 3. Indirect Object | Your boss gave *the fact that you came to this course* her undivided attention. |
| 4. Object of a Preposition | The reason for your success is found in *the fact that you came to this course.* |
| 5. Object of a Verbal Phrase | Emphasizing *the fact that you came to this course,* your boss gave you a raise. |
| 6. Appositive | In authorizing your Christmas bonus, your boss stressed one thing, *the fact that you came to this course.* |
| 7. Subject Complement | The reason you succeeded was *the fact that you came to this course.* |
| 8. Object Complement | We pronounced the worse clause in the English language *the fact that you came to this course.* [This is the only example of an object complement I've been able to discover. It doesn't really work, functioning instead more like an appositive.] |

There. The same noun clause can run through the language in eight ways just like any noun. And what made that bunch of words a clause? The two words: *you came.* The main verb *came* formed a dependent clause. And how might we *un*form a clause? By taking away its verb.

We'll come back to the art of clause-cutting. But first, a visit with the other two kinds of dependent clauses: adjective and adverb clauses.

### The Adjective Clause

The adjective clause is one of the most frequently used clauses in expository writing. Despite its prevalence, the clause invariably confuses many writers and forces them into unnecessary mistakes. The mistakes become not only grammatical embarrassments but also disasters in logic and meaning. For here we discuss the most notorious of all clauses:

### That and Which Clauses

Let's begin with some definitions. An adjective clause is *a bunch of words with a main verb in it* that modifies a noun. It functions just like a single-word adjective. It shows the character, kind, shape, size, quantity, uniqueness, or other trait of the modified noun.

Though it functions just like a single-word adjective, the adjective clause does have one unique feature distinguishing it from a single-word adjective. A single-word adjective typically precedes the word it modifies. (The only exceptions are the predicate adjective or adjective appositive, which can follow the words they modify.) An adjective clause, on the other hand, always must follow the word it modifies.

Keep in mind that an adjective clause is modifying a noun in your sentence. Also keep in mind that nouns are persons, places, things, or ideas. Your readers often want to know more about the nouns you include in your sentences. Often they'll want to know *which one* you're talking about. If your noun is a *department*, they might want to know *which department*. If your noun is a *rule*, they might want to know *which rule*. If your noun is a *factor*, they might want to know *which factor*. Or if your noun is a *red Porsche*, they might want to know *which red Porsche*. Keep the *which one* question in mind. The notion of it becomes crucial as we proceed.

An adjective clause, therefore, is describing a particular noun in your sentence. The clause will usually begin with one of these words:

| | |
|---|---|
| that | whom |
| which | whose |
| who | |

Here are some examples of adjective clauses:

I always buy his books *that receive rave reviews.*

I always buy his books, *which receive rave reviews.*

The candidate *who runs the best race* usually wins.

Mr. Keyes, *whom we all admire*, will address the convention.

The case, *whose decision started a revolution in products liability law*, prompted radical changes in the way manufacturers package their goods.

Other words, it should be noted, also may introduce an adjective clause. The subordinating conjunctions *where* and *when* often fit quite nicely: At the time *when Columbus discovered America*, the art of navigation was quite primitive. Or: In New York, *where Mayor Koch rules with an iron glove*, the press often has a field day. The clauses that typically cause the trouble, however, are the *that* and *which* clauses.

What causes all the trouble with adjective clauses? Two things: (1) choosing the correct relative pronoun and (2) deciding on the correct punctuation. Understanding these two issues requires your thoroughly understanding the differences between *restrictive* and *nonrestrictive* clauses.

Back in 1975, when I was serving as the Director of Legal Writing at the University of Virginia School of Law, I remember reading a book written by a noted law professor. In that book, the professor sometimes used *that* and other times used *which*. I looked and looked for some slight difference in meaning. Finding none, I consulted my unabridged dictionary, looked up *that*, and discovered:

*That: a relative pronoun used to introduce a restrictive clause.*

Thanks a bunch. Flipping back to the *w's* I looked up *which* and found:

*Which: a relative pronoun used to introduce a nonrestrictive clause.*

Terrific. Trying another approach I found *restrictive clause* defined:

> *A restrictive clause is a defining clause necessary to the meaning*
> *of the sentence.*

Wonderful. Undaunted but teeth clenched, I skipped over to the *n's* and checked out *nonrestrictive clause.* You guessed it:

> *A nonrestrictive clause is a nondefining clause unnecessary to the*
> *meaning of the sentence.*

Whoopie. Why couldn't one of these Ph.D.-types *explain* anything?

I searched the halls of academe for some soul who knew the difference between *that* and *which.* I found one such professor, and his discussion of the differences between these two words and the differences between restrictive and nonrestrictive clauses has stuck with me to this day. I'll share it with you in the hope that these vital differences stay with you as well.

Let's set up a sample clause and show you this professor's approach to *that-which identification.* Here's my clause:

> I always buy his books *that receive rave reviews.*

Here's the professor's approach. Focus your attention on the noun you're modifying. Here we're modifying the noun *books.* How many books has he written? Presumably a whole slew. Do I buy all his books? No, I just buy the ones that receive rave reviews. I do not buy all the other ones that receive bad reviews. I would not even buy those that receive mediocre reviews. I only buy the ones that receive rave reviews.

So I ask myself this question: *Which* group of books? *That* group of books. A restrictive *that* clause is *defining* which books I mean. Out of all the books that he has written, which ones do I buy? Those *that* receive rave reviews.

A restrictive *that* clause is a finger-pointer. A singler-outer. The clause is singling out one or a group among many. Which one? Which group? Which noun? Which books? That one. That group. That noun. That group of books. Not all the others. *That* one. Ironically, a *that* clause answers the question: *which one?*

Now let's use the same clause but make it nonrestrictive:

> I always buy his books, *which receive rave reviews.*

Here's the professor's approach. Focus your attention on the noun you're modifying. Here we're modifying the noun *books*. How many books has he written? Presumably a whole slew. Do I buy all of his books? Yes. And guess what? All receive rave reviews. I do buy all his books. None receives a bad or mediocre review. There is not one book he has written that I do not buy.

A nonrestrictive *which* clause is not a finger-pointer. Not a singler-outer. The information in the clause merely adds information about the modified noun. It does not single out the modified noun. The reader already knows *which one* or *which group*. The reader does not need the information in the clause for the sentence to make sense. Of most importance, the nonrestrictive clause *must* be set off by commas from the rest of the sentence. The nonrestrictive clause *must* be introduced by the word *which* and never by the word *that*.

Unfortunately, these days it is also proper to use *which* as the restrictive relative pronoun. It is proper to say: *I always buy his books which receive rave reviews*. That sentence, without the commas, means that I buy only those books that receive rave reviews and not those that receive bad or mediocre reviews. Thus, there are some of his books that I do not buy.

I say "unfortunately" for a very good reason. We had such a good system going. *That* meant restrictive, and *which* meant nonrestrictive. If everyone knew the difference, then no one's meaning ever could be confused.

I have it on good authority that *that's* don't sound too intelligent. Professors, therefore, and other real smart people decided to declare war on *that's* and to use *which's* instead. (Have you ever noticed that professors rarely say *that*? Instead they like to use lots of *which's*. Perhaps that explains all the mistakes they make with restrictive and nonrestrictive clauses.) Because of this conspiracy, the rest of us mortals must now cope with dual relative pronouns *that/which* can introduce restrictive clauses.

The importance of punctuation, therefore, becomes paramount. The nonrestrictive clause must be set off by commas. The restrictive clause must never be set off by commas.

Ordinarily, I advise writers to use *that* to introduce restrictive clauses and *which* to introduce nonrestrictive clauses. In one situation, however, use of *which* is mandatory for a restrictive clause, for *which* will permit a preceding preposition while *that* will not. If you refuse to end a clause with a preposition, then you must use *which* as the restrictive relative. Consider this example:

> The books that I told you about have arrived at the store.

Now that's a grammatically correct sentence. And, no, there's nothing wrong with ending a sentence or a clause with a preposition. You've heard the old Winston Churchill story? Arguing with a stuck-up grammarian about whether one could end a sentence or clause with a preposition, Churchill snarled:

> "My friend, that's an arcane rule of grammar up with which I shall not put."

That ended that.

But in formal writing, you might not want to end a sentence or clause with a preposition. To avoid ending the above clause with a preposition, you must use *which* as the restrictive relative pronoun as follows:

> The books about which I told you have arrived at the store.

Before moving on to the adverb clause, I should make two additional comments about the pronouns introducing adjective clauses. First, if the noun modified is a person, then ordinarily you must use either *who* or *whom* or *whose* to introduce the clause. You can decide on the proper *case* of the pronoun by using the following trick. The case must be subjective (who) if the main verb in the clause does not have some other subject. Thus: The candidate *who runs the best race* usually wins. Here the main verb of the clause *runs* does not have its own subject. It needs a subject. The relative pronoun will serve as its subject. It must be in the subjective case. The correct word is *who*.

If, on the other hand, the main verb in the clause already has some other subject, it cannot have yet another one. Indeed, the clause is really yearning for an object. The relative pronoun fills this need for an object. It must be in the objective case (whom). Thus: Mr. Keyes, *whom we all admire,* will address the convention. The main verb of the clause *admire* has its own subject *we*. It cannot have another subject. It needs an object. The correct word, in the objective case, is *whom*.

If the noun you modify is a generic type of person, however, you may use *that* as the relative. Thus: The candidate *that runs the best race* usually wins.

Second, to avoid awkward *of which* constructions, you may use the personal pronoun *whose* even though the noun modified is not a person. Thus: The case, *whose decision started a revolution in products liability law,* prompted radical changes in the way manufacturers package their goods. That sentence is preferable to: The case, *the decision of which started a revolution in products liability law,* prompted radical changes in the way manufacturers package their goods.

Now, before learning to cut some of these clauses, let's look quickly at the final type of clause—the adverb clause.

### The Adverb Clause

The adverb clause modifies the main verb of the independent clause to which it is attached. Or it might modify the entire sentence, as adverbs often do. Keep in mind that adverbs answer the following questions about the verbs they modify: *when, where, how,* and *why.* To gain precision in language, you should try to choose the *clause starter* that most precisely answers the adverbial question you intend. Here, again, is a partial list of adverb *clause starters*, also called *subordinating conjunctions*:

Subordinating Conjunctions

| | |
|---|---|
| after | insofar as |
| although | like |
| as | since |
| as long as | though |
| as soon as | when |
| as well as | where |
| because | whereas |
| before | whether |
| even though | while |
| if | |

Adverb clauses actually cause little trouble in writing style. If anything, writers probably don't use enough adverb clauses. The reason is simple. As we've seen in previous chapters, writers have forgotten the action verb. If they don't use many action verbs, then they don't use many adverb clauses. They just don't have many verbs to modify.

### The Art of Clause-Cutting

The biggest deal in the English language is the main verb. It, and it alone, distinguishes a clause as a clause. The main verb forms the independent clause. Along with its subject, the main verb forms the milestone of every sentence. On this milestone hang all other sentence parts: adjectives, adverbs, prepositional phrases, verbal phrases, appositives, adverb clauses, adjective clauses, noun clauses, and a host of others.

The big-deal main verb also forms the dependent clause. The main verb forms the noun clause, serving any one of the eight noun functions. The main verb forms the adjective clause, modifying nouns in a restrictive or nonrestrictive way. The main verb forms the adverb clause, modifying the verb of the independent clause.

Because the main verb is such a big deal, you should be careful in building clauses. You need at least one independent clause for each sentence. On it you can hang a multitude of big-deal dependent clauses. If you hang too many clauses on a single sentence, however, all sorts of horribles come about. The sentence becomes long-winded. The sentence has too many subordinate thoughts. The sentence has so many big deals that it detracts from those messages that truly are big deals.

The powerful writer must learn to cut clauses. The art of cutting the clause and the product left over after the cutting is done vary with the type of clause. That's why I spent most of this chapter reintroducing you to noun clauses, adjective clauses, and adverb clauses. To learn to cut them, we'll deal with noun clauses separately and adverb and adjective clauses together.

### Cutting Noun Clauses

What's a clause? A bunch of words with a main verb in it. When the clause is a noun clause, it satisfies the meaning of a noun in the sentence. In short, a noun clause uses a main verb to satisfy the meaning of a noun.

Does all this sound familiar? In Chapter 3, we explored the irony of using derivative nouns and derivative adjectives to satisfy the meaning of a verb. When a sentence begged for a verb, we learned to give it a verb. If the sentence wants to say *the agency concluded*, why should we say *the agency reached a conclusion*? That sentence wanted a verb. Give it one.

Now the shoe is on the other foot. Now we must look at situations where sentences are pleading for nouns. They are on bended knee. They pine for a noun form. When does a sentence beg for a noun? Whenever you begin a grammatical structure that needs one of the eight noun functions to complete it, your sentence will beg for a noun. For example, if you use a preposition, then your sentence needs a noun to complete the prepositional phrase. If you use a transitive verb, then your sentence is begging for a noun to act as the object. What do awkward and verbose writers do to the poor, pleading sentence? You got it. They deny it the noun. They give it a main verb. They give it an awkward noun clause.

If you have lots of *that's* and *the fact that's* in your writing, you are a prime candidate for some serious exercise in the art of noun clause-cutting. Pay attention. Cutting noun clauses requires a rather sophisticated grammatical analysis. Fortunately, no more 10-minute grammar lessons are needed at this point. Everything you need to know has already been covered.

To have some examples to work with, let's go back to our *the fact that* clauses that we ran through all eight noun functions. Here are the first seven again (I've omitted the object complement, which was kind of bogus anyway):

| Seven Noun Functions | Italicized Example |
|---|---|
| 1. Subject | *The fact that you came to this course* shows your interest in clear writing. |
| 2. Direct Object | Your boss applauded *the fact that you came to this course.* |
| 3. Indirect Object | Your boss gave *the fact that you came to this course* her undivided attention. |
| 4. Object of a Preposition | The reason for your success is found in *the fact that you came to this course.* |

| | |
|---|---|
| 5. Object of a Verbal Phrase | Emphasizing *the fact that you came to this course,* your boss gave you a raise. |
| 6. Appositive | In authorizing your Christmas bonus, your boss stressed one thing, *the fact that you came to this course.* |
| 7. Subject Complement | The reason you succeeded was *the fact that you came to this course.* |

All these sentences are pleading for revision. All they want is a noun—a subject, a direct object, an indirect object, an object of a preposition, and so on. Instead, the wordy writer satisfies this need for a noun with a main verb. The careful writer recognizes this anomaly and cuts the noun clause. Here are the two tricks of cutting noun clauses. First of all, identify the main verb in the noun clause as either (1) not the verb *to be* or (2) the verb *to be.* Then use the *not "to be" trick* or the *"to be" trick.*

### Noun Clause-Cutting Trick #1

*Not "To Be"—The Similar Noun Approach.*
If the verb is not the verb *to be,* then look for a similar noun meaning the same thing as the verb form.

*Not "To Be"—The Gerund Approach.*
If the verb is not the verb *to be* and if you cannot find a suitable noun substitute, try adding *-ing* to the main verb. Its present participial form can act as a gerund and satisfy the "noun urge" that your sentence is begging for.

Because the verb in our sample noun clause above is not the verb *to be,* let's try converting the main verb by using the *similar noun approach* and the *gerund approach.* Though either one works, I tend to favor the *similar noun* solution for our sample noun clause.

In our example, the similar noun form *your attendance at this course* means the same as the main verb form *the fact that you came to this course.* Try the noun substitute. Not having any verb, the clause will go away. If the noun substitute sounds better and less awkward, then use it.

| Seven Noun Functions | Similar Noun Approach |
|---|---|
| 1. Subject | *Your attendance at this course* shows your interest in clear writing. |
| 2. Direct Object | Your boss applauded *your attendance at this course.* |
| 3. Indirect Object | Your boss gave *your attendance at this course* her undivided attention. |
| 4. Object of a Preposition | The reason for your success is found in *your attendance at this course.* |
| 5. Object of a Verbal Phrase | Emphasizing *your attendance at this course*, your boss gave you a raise. |
| 6. Appositive | In authorizing your Christmas bonus, your boss stressed one thing, *your attendance at this course.* |
| 7. Subject Complement | The reason you succeeded was *your attendance at this course.* |

Now for the *gerund approach.* In our examples, the gerund form *your coming to this course* means the same as the main verb form *the fact that you came to this course.* If the gerund fits, sounds better, and feels less awkward, then use it. Here are the same examples above:

| Seven Noun Functions | Gerund Approach |
|---|---|
| 1. Subject | *Your coming to this course* shows your interest in clear writing. |
| 2. Direct Object | Your boss applauded *your coming to this course.* |
| 3. Indirect Object | Your boss gave *your coming to this course* her undivided attention. |

| 4. Object of a Preposition | The reason for your success is found in *your coming to this course.* |
| 5. Object of a Verbal Phrase | Emphasizing *your coming to this course,* your boss gave you a raise. |
| 6. Appositive | In authorizing your Christmas bonus, your boss stressed one thing, *your coming to this course.* |
| 7. Subject Complement | The reason you succeeded was *your coming to this course.* |

### A Special Note on the Gerund Approach

If you use gerunds to avoid noun clauses—and many top writers do—you must be careful when you modify the gerund with a personal pronoun. If you need to modify the gerund, be sure to use the possessive case of that personal pronoun. If you use the subjective or objective case, your meaning will change completely. Consider these examples.

You spend Saturday night with Mom. On Sunday morning she gets up and begins frying chicken. The aroma awakens you. You come into the kitchen and correctly say:

"I smelled your frying chicken."

That's right. You smelled the *frying. Frying* served the noun function as direct object of the transitive verb *smelled.* The case of the personal pronoun, in order to modify the gerund-noun, had to be possessive. Many people, however, would make a dramatic mistake and say:

"I smelled you frying chicken."

That's incorrect. The *you* in the objective case changes the meaning. *You,* in the objective case, becomes the direct object of *smelled.* Now you are smelling *you. Frying chicken* becomes a present participial phrase modifying *you.* Mom, of course, is miffed and will likely clean your clock with a skillet upside the head.

The same kind of mistake can occur with other nouns used to modify the gerund. Consider how the meaning shifts in the two examples below. In the first, the lobbyist is aware of the *Senate*. In the second, the lobbyist is aware of the *passing*.

> The lobbyist is aware of the Senate passing the Clean Harbor Act.

> The lobbyist is aware of the Senate's passing the Clean Harbor Act.

Now let's use the noun clause-cutting technique when the main verb in the clause *is* the verb *to be*. Here's the second trick.

### Noun Clause-Cutting Trick #2

*"To Be" + Predicate Adjective—Similar Noun Approach.*
If the verb in the clause is the verb *to be*, it will probably be followed by a predicate adjective or a predicate nominative. If a predicate adjective is present, you can often find a similar noun, which, when used, will obliterate the clause.

*"To Be" + Predicate Nominative—the "Status" Approach.*
If the verb *to be* is followed by a noun, there's not a whole lot you can do to get rid of the clause. One solution I've been able to devise is to use the noun *status*, which provides an approximate noun form for the verb *to be*. Sometimes, of course, you can make *to be* a gerund (*being*) to obliterate a noun clause.

Here are some examples of these two approaches to noun clause-cutting.

| *To Be* Noun Clauses | Proposed Revisions |
|---|---|
| The boss emphasized the fact that the employee was tardy. | The boss emphasized the employee's tardiness. |
| Congress was aware of the fact that he was President. | Congress was aware of his status as President. |

### Writing as Good Writers Write

Do good writers use the noun clause-cutting device? Without doubt. Consider the Justice Black example in Chapter 1. Here's one of his sentences:

The Framers knew, better perhaps than we do today, the risks
they were taking.

Mr. Justice Black's sentence was begging for a noun. His transitive
verb *knew* yearned for a direct object. He could have satisfied that noun
need with a noun clause like this:

The Framers knew, better perhaps than we do today, that they
were taking risks.

But knowing that noun clauses often are tongue-twisters, he went
ahead and gave the sentence a noun—*risks*—and modified it with an
adjective clause—*they were taking.*

Each day when I pick up a national newspaper or magazine, I will
find examples of the rule: *When a sentence wants a noun, give it a noun.*
A few years back, when the movie *The Right Stuff* premiered in
Washington, I read the following sentence in *The Washington Post*:

I dredge up, with some glee, Washington's losing its mind over
the premiere of *The Right Stuff*.

I was struck by what the writer did not say:

I dredge up, with some glee, the fact that Washington is losing
its mind over the premiere of the *The Right Stuff*.

I dredge up, with some glee, Washington's loss of its mind over
the premiere of *The Right Stuff*.

The first has an awkward noun clause. The *similar noun approach*
to cutting the noun clause in the second fails to convey the expression
*losing one's mind.* The *gerund approach* to cutting the noun clause seems
to work best.

The bottom line? Learn the eight noun functions. Watch for them
as they inevitably play out in your sentences. Learn to satisfy these noun
urges with noun forms. When you truly need the main-verb meaning,
then use the noun clause. But if a true noun form states your meaning
best, use it. Your writing, as a result, will achieve a natural grace.

### Cutting Adjective and Adverb Clauses

Writing with too many clauses clutters up your prose. Above we
saw how to cut noun clauses by substituting true nouns or noun forms

to satisfy the noun function of the clause. Now let's turn our attention to the other two kinds of dependent clauses, the adjective and adverb clauses. Because these clauses serve the same function of *modifying,* we can deal with them together.

As you know, adjectives modify nouns. Adjective clauses also modify nouns. Adverbs primarily modify verbs, although they can modify other adverbs, adjectives, or entire sentences. The adverb clause, however, typically modifies either the main verb in the independent clause or the entire sentence.

The trick in cutting unnecessary clauses is to find some other structure that will serve the adjective or adverb function of the clause you're cutting. The question thus becomes: *What else in the English language can serve as adjectives and adverbs?* The answer readily comes to mind. We can cut clauses down to adjectives, adverbs, prepositional phrases, verbal phrases, adjective appositives, noun appositives, absolutes, and truncated adverb clauses. Examples will show the trick in action:

### Cut Clause Down to Adjective

The agency considered the issues *which were vital.*

The agency considered the *vital* issues.

### Cut Clause Down to Adverb

*There are instances in which* consumers are abused by false advertising.

Consumers are *sometimes* abused by false advertising.

### Cut Clause Down to Prepositional Phrase

*While the meeting was in progress,* the managers excluded the summer interns.

*During the meeting,* the managers excluded the summer interns.

### Cut Clause Down to Verbal Phrase

Remember Mr. Justice Cardozo's paragraph in the *Palsgraf* case. Guess which one he used? Clause or verbal phrase?

| | |
|---|---|
| The other man, *who was carrying a package,* jumped aboard the car . . . . | The other man, *carrying a package,* jumped aboard the car . . . . |

Here's another example:

| | |
|---|---|
| The statute, *which was enacted in the 1960s,* dramatically expanded our civil rights. | The statute, *enacted in the 1960s,* dramatically expanded our civil rights. |

Here's another example:

| | |
|---|---|
| *If citizens are to obtain information,* they must file the proper request with the Agency's Freedom of Information Office. | *To obtain information,* citizens must file the proper request with the Agency's Freedom of Information Office. |

Each of these requires comment. The first (Cardozo) example: you can cut virtually every progressive tense clause to a present participial phrase. The second example: you can cut virtually every passive voice clause to a past participial phrase. Be very careful when using present or past participial phrases. If the phrase is nonrestrictive, it *must* be set off by commas. If the phrase is restrictive, it *must not* be set off by commas. In the first two examples, both phrases are nonrestrictive. They do not point out *which man* or *which statute*. From context the reader would already know *which man* or *which statute*. The third example: the clause is reduced to an infinitive phrase, an often effective way to convey hard-hitting verb meaning without the big deal of a clause.

### Cut Clause Down to Adjective Appositive

Adjective clauses having the verb *to be* followed by a predicate adjective can often be cut to a structure called the *adjective appositive*. You've already seen the noun appositive in our discussion of the eight noun functions. The adjective appositive is similar. Like the noun appositive, it follows the noun it modifies. Also like the noun appositive, it is set off by commas if nonrestrictive and is not set off by commas if restrictive. However, unlike the noun appositive, which can consist of just one word, the adjective appositive usually must have more than one word. Study this example, which shows a *to be* adjective clause cut down to an adjective appositive:

| The issues *that are pertinent to our inquiry* include the advisability of raising prices and the consequent effect on profits. | The issues *pertinent to our inquiry* include the advisability of raising prices and the consequent effect on profits. |

Do good writers use adjective appositives? In the following sentence, taken from Mr. Justice Black's passage, can you find the adjective appositive? Check out the last 14 words of the sentence:

> With this knowledge they still believed that the ultimate happiness and security of a nation lies in its ability to explore, to change, to grow and ceaselessly to adapt itself to a new knowledge born of inquiry free from any kind of governmental control over the mind and spirit of man.

### Cut Clause Down to Noun Appositive

The same clause-cutting device often produces noun appositives. You should check your writing to see if you use appositives at all. If you do not, the chances are good your writing is too *clausy*. Consider this example:

| The evidence contradicted the main witness, *who had been convicted of having committed a felony.* | The evidence contradicted the main witness, *a convicted felon.* |

### Cut Clause Down to Absolute

You might use *absolutes* without knowing you use them. If, after learning about them here, you find you don't use them at all, then try them out. They enable you to pack a lot of information in a small amount of space. An absolute is an incomplete sentence attached to a complete sentence; it has in it either a present participle, a past participle, or some other adjective modifying a noun; it must be set off by commas. The distinguishing feature of the absolute is the presence of the subject of the discarded clause. Note the retained subjects and adjectives in these examples:

| *His research was complete,* and he began to build his arguments. | *His research complete,* he began to build his arguments. |

| | |
|---|---|
| *Because the board had decided the issue,* the parties searched for ways to appeal. | *The board having decided the issue,* the parties searched for ways to appeal. |

### *Cut Clause Down to Truncated Adverb Clause*

The final product of clause-cutting is the *truncated adverb clause.* Like the absolute, it might not be familiar by name. You should search your writing for the structure, and not finding it, begin to use it. It, too, can pack information down into a tight, hard-hitting package.

The truncated adverb clause uses a subordinating conjunction with an unconjugated verb, typically a present participle or a past participle. Here are examples:

| | |
|---|---|
| *When it decides a case,* the court usually relies on precedent. | *When deciding a case,* the court usually relies on precedent. |
| *When it is finished,* the report is printed. | *When finished,* the report is printed. |
| *If it is deserved,* the victory is sweet. | *If deserved,* the victory is sweet. |

### That-Dropping

Finally, when any adjective clause has an independent subject of the main verb, you may, at your discretion, drop the *that* or *which* introducing the clause. If the adjective clause is short, dropping the *that* often produces a tighter, more effective style. If the adjective clause is long, however, it is usually best to retain the *that* to anchor the clause. Obviously, if the clause does not have an independent subject, the *that* or *which* (or *who*) is needed to serve as that subject. Here are some examples:

| | |
|---|---|
| The result *that we want* is total victory. | The result *we want* is total victory. |
| He likes the words *that start the clauses.* | He likes the words *that start the clauses.* |

Remember that the word *that* also starts noun clauses. When such clauses follow *cognitive* verbs, you should retain the *that.* Cognitive

verbs include *know, assume, learn, remember,* and many others. Hence:
I assume *that* you know *that* you are late.

Do good writers use *thats* after cognitive verbs? Here's Mr. Justice
Black, again:

> They *knew that* free speech might be the friend of change and
> revolution. But they also *knew that* it is always the deadliest
> enemy of tyranny. With this knowledge they still *believed that*
> the ultimate happiness and security of a nation lies in its ability
> to explore, to change, to grow and ceaselessly to adapt itself to
> a new knowledge born of inquiry free from any kind of
> governmental control over the mind and spirit of man.

### Summary

It's been a long chapter. I hope you've learned the vital role played
by the three dependent clauses—noun clauses, adjective clauses, and
adverb clauses. By now, you are familiar with those special words, the
*clause starters*, which set up dependent clauses. You know the subordinating conjunctions, which start adverb clauses; the relative pronouns,
which start adjective clauses; and those unnamed words that start noun
clauses.

Though the role of clauses is vital, too many clauses do clutter up
our language. Learning to cut clauses is one of the most important skills
the careful writer can acquire. Learning to cut requires an appreciation
of the byproduct of clause-cutting. You must know that noun clauses
convert to true or substitute nouns and that adjective and adverb clauses
convert to one of a variety of other adjective or adverb structures:
adjectives, adverbs, prepositional phrases, verbal phrases (present participial, past participial, and infinitive), adjective appositives, noun appositives, absolutes, and truncated adverb clauses.

That's clause-cutting. But before leaving clauses altogether, I'll
close by dispelling some popular clause myths.

### Three Strange Clause Myths

For some reason, over time, three strange myths have developed
about dependent clauses. Discussing these issues with some people can
be difficult. They tenaciously cling to lifelong beliefs, no matter how
persuasive the arguments against them. The myths are widespread. No
doubt you've heard about them yourself.

### Myth: Do Not Begin a Sentence with "Because"

I've talked with some highly qualified experts. They can't figure out where this myth came from. But many people believe that you *can't* begin a sentence with a *because clause*. Because they believe this myth so firmly, these people rob themselves of perfectly good, introductory adverb clauses. Because they forbid beginning a sentence with the *cause*, they fail to stress the *effect* by placing it at the end of the sentence. Because they single out the subordinating conjunction *because* for special treatment, they might even neglect ever to use an introductory adverb clause.

Can I not say what I just said in the preceding three sentences? If you say "no," then can I say the following?

If I were you, I'd join the club.

While he watched TV, he ate and ate and ate.

When the company raised prices, corporate profits plummeted.

Of course I can begin those sentences with adverb clauses. Of course I can use the subordinating conjunctions *if, while,* and *when* to begin a sentence. Why is the subordinating conjunction—*because*—any different? The answer? It's not.

### Myth: "Since" Never Means "Because"

The subordinating conjunction *since* does have a highly temporal meaning. As a rule, it's best to confine your use of *since* to show relationships in time. Thus:

Since he became of age, he has enjoyed the privileges of adulthood.

But some people believe that *since* never, ever can mean *because*. Of course it can. Here's the definition found in the dictionary:

For the reason that: because of the fact that (since it was raining, he wore a hat). (Webster's, p. 2122).

The best rule to follow is this: If your sentence using *since* to mean *because* could convey the temporal meaning of *since*, then use *because* to avoid the possible ambiguity. Suppose in the following example I really mean *because*. You can see the ambiguity resulting from the temporal meaning of *since* and the consequent need to use the word *because*.

> Since Reagan was elected and missles were deployed in Europe, the Soviets more readily bargained in the INF negotiations.

### Myth: "While" Never Means "Although"

The same analysis applies to our last clause myth. *While* also has a highly temporal meaning. But it can also mean *although, though,* or *even though*. Here's the dictionary definition:

> In spite of the fact that: although (while the evidence he has obtained may be said to fit the theory, the importance of some of it is questionable). (Webster's, p. 2604).

In deciding which word to use, follow the same rule that applies to *because*: If your sentence using *while* to mean *although* could convey the temporal meaning of *while*, then use *although* to avoid the possible ambiguity. In the following example, I mean *though*. Note the possible ambiguity.

> While the price of a barrel of oil declines, the price of a gallon of gas goes up.

Those are the three strange clause myths. And that's clause-cutting.

### The Rules of Good Writing

Your list of the rules of good writing now looks like this:

1. Use an average of 25 words per sentence.

2. Avoid putting too many messages in a single sentence.

3. Put most of your messages at the subject-predicate position.

4. For variety or emphasis, invert your sentences.

5. Use the art of subordination to smooth out choppiness.

6. Avoid disrupting your sentences with thought-stopping gaps.

7. Watch out for the rule of parallel construction.

8. Tabulate particularly complex information.

9. Hammer home your point with the powerful, versatile verb.

10. Use the verb *to be* only when you mean it.

11. Get rid of compound prepositions.

12. Cut adjective, adverb, and noun clauses to other structures satisfying the same functions.

On to the Great Debate, the Active vs. the Passive Voice.

---

*References*

W. Strunk & E. White, *The Elements of Style* (3d ed. 1979).

*Webster's Third New International Dictionary* (Merriam-Webster, Inc. 1981).

# Chapter 7

# The Great Debate
# Active vs. Passive Voice

*It was decided that a meeting would be held.*

—Letter from a federal official.

# Chapter 7

## The Great Debate

## Active vs. Passive Voice

### Introduction

One day in 1975, shortly after I took charge of the writing program at U.Va., I was enjoying a cup of coffee in the faculty lounge. As I was reading my *Washington Post*, I heard a well-known law professor say the following: "I never use the passive voice. I always use the active voice."

My heart pounded. As the new "resident expert," I was about to be asked to join the conversation. I slid down in my seat and raised my *Post* for protection. That was one conversation I had to avoid. For the life of me, I couldn't recall the precise differences between the active voice and the passive voice. Certainly I didn't remember enough nuances to join the level of conversation expected in the faculty lounge.

When the moment was right, I sprinted for the door, made a beeline for my office, and grabbed the closest grammar guide I could find. I began to bone up. I began to study the difference. I learned all about the bad reputation of the passive voice and the many reactions against it. I got to the point where I could detect the passive voice in patterns of speech.

In the faculty lounge, it's too bad the subject never came up again.

Through the years, I've encountered several strange events concerning the passive voice. First, I saw a memorandum from the head of a federal government agency:

To:     All Employees
From: Name Deleted
Re:     The Passive Voice

The passive voice is used exclusively in the federal government.
[The memo continued to criticize the passive voice and strongly suggest that employees avoid it entirely.]

Second, the head of one of the federal departments outlawed the passive voice from all correspondence going out over his signature. Third, a magazine article on clear writing urged that "the passive voice should be avoided."

There's a much better way to deal with this great debate. Joining the hysteria to rant and rave against the passive voice will educate no one. Instead, a sense of balance is definitely in order. Thus, in this chapter, I'll back up to square one and assume that you aren't exactly sure of the precise differences between the active voice and the passive voice. We'll learn that *voice* pertains only to transitive verbs. We'll study the differences between the active voice and the passive voice. Then, and only then, we'll learn not only to prefer the active voice but to avoid a knee-jerk reaction against the passive voice and instead to use it to our advantage.

### Verbs: Transitive or Intransitive

Before learning the differences between the active and the passive voice, you must first recall the differences between transitive and intransitive verbs. Transitive verbs are *action verbs* that carry action from the subject of the sentence to the direct object—the recipient of the action. Put another way, a transitive verb is an action verb capable of being followed by a noun. Put yet another way, a transitive verb is an action verb that is begging for a noun to follow it. Here are some examples:

| Subject | Transitive Verb | Direct Object |
|---|---|---|
| John | hit | the ball. |
| The agency | decided | the issue. |
| The manager | hired | the employee. |

To test whether a verb is transitive or intransitive, just plug in the verb and ask this question: *Can I [verb] something or somebody?* If the answer is "yes," then the verb is transitive. Thus, I can hit something (or somebody), decide something, or hire somebody.

Before using the test on some verbs, let's examine the other kind of verb, the intransitive verb. The intransitive verb is also an *action verb*. It does not, however, *carry action* from a subject to a direct object. Indeed, the intransitive verb cannot be followed by a noun. It cannot have a direct object. Applying the *can I verb something* test, you will always answer "no." An intransitive verb, therefore, does not have a direct object. The intransitive verb does not beg for a noun. Rather, it typically begs for an adverb.

Thus, consider the verb *walk*. Apply the test: *Can I walk something?* Typically the answer is "no." I do not walk some*thing*. Rather, I walk somehow, somewhere, sometime, or for some reason. The verb begs not for a noun, but for an adverb or adverbial phrase:

I walk quickly (somehow).

I walk to the store (somewhere).

I walk on Sundays (sometime).

I walk for exercise (for some reason).

Another *question test* is helpful in classifying a verb as transitive or intransitive. You can follow a transitive verb with a *what* or a *whom* question. Try this: *[verb] what?* or *[verb] whom?* If this question makes sense, the verb is transitive. Thus: *hit what?* or *decide what?* or *hire whom?* All those questions make sense. Notice that the questions are *noun* questions. These action verbs want nouns. They want direct objects.

On the other hand, you can follow an intransitive verb with four different questions: *how, where, when,* or *why.* Note that these questions are adverbial.

walk how (quickly)

walk where (to the store)

walk when (on Sundays)

walk why (for exercise)

All those questions make sense as well.

Parenthetically, I do not mean to imply that you cannot adverbially modify a transitive verb. Of course you can hit the ball *out of the park,* decide the case *quickly,* or hire the employee *without much thought of the consequences.* The point I make is this: a transitive verb wants a noun whereas an intransitive verb is searching for an adverb.

Let's use the above tests to classify some verbs as transitive, intransitive, or both. First, the verb *walk*. As noted above, typically you do not walk *something*. Instead, you walk *how, where, when*, or *why*. But if you take the dog along, you can *walk the dog*. In this sense, *walk* is transitive. Similarly, you could *walk a refrigerator up the stairs*. Let's try some others:

1. *Comply*. Can you *comply something*? No. You comply *with* something. The verb, therefore, is intransitive.

2. *Provide*. Can you *provide something*? Yes. As a transitive verb, *provide* means to furnish, to afford, or to stipulate. But you can also provide *for* something. The verb is also intransitive. As an intransitive verb, *provide* means to take measures in advance (as in *to provide for the common defense*) or to furnish subsistence (as in *to provide for his family's needs*).

3. *Delve*. Can you *delve something*? No. You delve *into* something. The verb is intransitive.

4. *Impact*. I just couldn't resist including the favorite word of the 1980s. Not only do people misuse it, but they have magically transformed the verb from the transitive verb that it is to the intransitive verb that it isn't. *Impact*, according to the dictionary, is a transitive verb. Guess what it means? *To strike with great force*. A good synonym would be *to nuke*. The example given in the dictionary: *The antitank missiles impacted the target area*. Yet people these days use this verb to mean *to affect*. Listen carefully and you'll hear somebody say, "We must decide whether our policies will impact the economy." Folks, if there's the slightest chance of your policies *blowing away* or *nuking* the economy, I sincerely hope you'll do away with the policies.

   The verb *impact* is transitive. It is therefore incorrect to say: "We must decide whether our policies will impact *on* the economy."

Before you can possibly understand the differences between the active and the passive voice, you must first learn to spot transitive verbs. The reason is simple: you can use transitive verbs either in the active voice or the passive voice. *Voice* has nothing to do with intransitive verbs. There's only one way to say *I walked to the store*. Thus, from this day forward, every time you use any transitive verb, you've got a decision to make—to put the verb in the active voice or the passive voice. Undoubtedly, most writers don't really choose a voice. Instead, they write habitually. The careful writer, the powerful writer, strategically chooses voice to achieve a particular objective.

### Voice of Transitive Verbs

Whatever one says in the active voice, I can translate into the passive voice. Watch. *Whatever is said in the active voice can be translated into the passive voice.* I just did it. *It was just done.*

You can conjugate every transitive verb in two ways: in the active voice or in the passive voice. *Every transitive verb can be conjugated in two ways* . . . I'd better stop this now . . . *This had better be stopped. . .* enough! Let's look carefully at each—the active voice and the passive voice.

### *The Active Voice*

In the active voice, the actor precipitates the action. The active-voice verb then carries that action to the recipient of the action, the direct object. Thus, in popular legal parlance:

| Actor | Action | Actee |
|-------|--------|-------|
| John | hits | the ball. |

Notice in the active voice that the action flows left to right. Indeed, in the active voice, we encounter the words in the same order as the represented action would unfold: *John,* the batter, steps up, takes a swing, and *hits* a round sphere we call *the ball.*

### *The Passive Voice*

In the passive voice, the sentence flip-flops. The recipient of the action becomes the grammatical subject of the sentence. The actor, the precipitator of the action, is revealed at the end of the sentence, usually as the object of a prepositional *by* phrase. Take a look:

| Actee | Action | Actor |
|-------|--------|-------|
| The ball | is hit | by John. |

Notice in the passive voice everything is backwards. We see the result or consequences or recipient of the action first. We then see the action. And finally we're introduced to the culprit—the whodunit—at the tail end of the sentence.

We can now understand the definitions of *active voice* and *passive voice.* The definitions derive from the grammatical subjects of the respective sentences. In the active voice, the subject of the sentence is active. In the passive voice, the subject of the sentence is passive. In the active voice, John—the subject—actively does the hitting. In the passive voice, the ball—the subject—passively sits there and gets hit.

Forming the active voice, of course, is a piece of cake. Just conjugate the verb in the twelve major tenses. Here's a third-person conjugation of the transitive verb *show* in the twelve major tenses:

| | |
|---|---|
| Present | John shows the movie. |
| Past | John showed the movie. |
| Future | John will show the movie. |
| Present Perfect | John has shown the movie. |
| Past Perfect | John had shown the movie. |
| Future Perfect | John will have shown the movie. |
| Present Progressive | John is showing the movie. |
| Past Progressive | John was showing the movie. |
| Future Progressive | John will be showing the movie. |
| Present Perfect Progressive | John has been showing the movie. |
| Past Perfect Progressive | John had been showing the movie. |
| Future Perfect Progressive | John will have been showing the movie. |

Adding various auxiliary verbs produces an almost endless array of possible verb meanings—all in the active voice: John *might have been showing* the movie. John *must show* the movie. John *could have shown* the movie.

### Forming the Passive Voice: *To Be* + Past Participle

Look at the progressive tenses shown above. They are formed by conjugating the auxiliary verb *to be* and adding the present participle. The passive voice is quite similar in structure. You form the passive voice by conjugating the verb *to be* and adding the *past* participle of the transitive verb.

The first hurdle is identifying the past participle of every transitive verb in the English language. You might protest that you don't remember all past participles of all transitive verbs in the English language. And I respond that you probably do know most past participles of most verbs in the English language. You know them because you routinely use them in the *perfect tenses*. To identify any past participle, just complete this sentence: *I have [plug in the past participle]*. Try it with these verbs:

| Transitive Verb | I have | Past Participle |
|---|---|---|
| show | I have | shown. |
| decide | I have | decided. |
| see | I have | seen. |
| ride | I have | ridden. |
| write | I have | written. |

To form the passive voice, follow this formula: *to be* + past participle of transitive verb = passive voice of the transitive verb. Here is the same transitive verb *show* conjugated in the passive voice in most of the twelve major tenses:

| | |
|---|---|
| Present | The movie is shown by John. |
| Past | The movie was shown by John. |
| Future | The movie will be shown by John. |
| Present Perfect | The movie has been shown by John. |
| Past Perfect | The movie had been shown by John. |
| Future Perfect | The movie will have been shown by John. |
| Present Progressive | The movie is being shown by John. |
| Past Progressive | The movie was being shown by John. |
| Future Progressive | None. |
| Present Perfect Progressive | None. |
| Past Perfect Progressive | None. |
| Future Perfect Progressive | None. |

Notice that the progressive tenses have only two passive voice constructions. The other four make no sense: *The movie "will be being shown" by John*?

Notice also that all passive constructions are formed by tacking on the past participle to some form of the verb *to be*. Just as we can form almost endless verb meanings in the active voice by using auxiliary verbs, so too can we form similar meanings in the passive voice: *The movie can be shown.* The movie *must be shown.* The movie *ought to have been shown.*

Remember infinitive phrases? Here's one in the active voice: *To show the movie* was John's goal in life. Here's one in the passive voice: *To be shown the movie* was the children's goal in life. Remember present participial phrases? Here's one in the active voice: *Showing the movie,* John charged an admission fee. Here's one in the passive voice: *Being shown the movie,* the children paid an admission fee. Virtually every active voice construction has a corresponding passive voice construction. And vice versa. Which will it be? Active or passive?

### Three Strikes Against the Passive Voice

As noted above, the passive voice has a very bad reputation. Style books love to say terrible things about the passive voice or to extol the virtues of the active voice. When praising the active voice, some experts even rely on the passive. Strunk and White observed:

> Many a tame sentence of description or exposition *can be made* lively and emphatic by substituting a transitive in the active voice for some such perfunctory expression as "there is" or "could be heard." (Strunk & White, p. 18, emphasis added).

Or they said:

> The need of making a particular word the subject of the sentence will often, as in these examples, determine which voice is *to be used.* (Strunk & White, p. 18, emphasis added).

Is this preference for the active voice valid? Is the bad reputation of the passive voice deserved? Yes, to both questions. The passive voice has three strikes against it. First, in the passive voice it takes more words to say the same thing:

John hit the ball (active, 4 words).

The ball was hit by John (passive, 6 words).

Second, the passive voice is, by definition, passive. It's weak. It's wimpy. Use the passive voice exclusively and you'll produce a string of sentences where no subject acts. Every grammatical subject just sits there and gets acted upon. Every subject sits there and takes it. Nothing ever seems to *happen* in the passive voice. Third, the passive voice is potentially irresponsible. Only in the passive voice can the writer cover up *whodunit* without obviously covering up. Watch this. Here's the passive voice: *The ball was hit.* Now here's the same sentence in the active voice: *Somebody hit the ball.* In the active voice, concealing the actor is obvious. In the passive, the coverup is more subtle.

Nowhere is the passive voice more tyrannical than in the press and in the government. Consider the Dan Quayle affair. Here's the press (quoted from a report by CBS's Dan Rather):

> Tonight, questions are being asked about J. Danforth Quayle's military experience in the National Guard.

Here's the active voice translation:

> Tonight, my colleagues in the press and I are asking questions about J. Danforth Quayle's military experience in the National Guard.

The government official, of course, uses the same trick. Here's Mr. Quayle's response to accusations about his service in the National Guard:

> Calls to the National Guard office were made.

Here's the active voice translation:

> My family and my contacts made calls to the National Guard office.

If you want to detect when someone else is fudging, covering-up, or hemming and hawing, watch for their use of the passive voice. It'll give them away every time.

Most of all, this biggest strike against the passive voice—its irresponsible nature—accounts for its popularity in organizations. Maybe policies and decisions do indeed unaccountably bubble out of an organization. Maybe decisions *are made.* Maybe *it was decided* that your petition for review *would be denied.* Perhaps *it was thought* that the policy *should be developed* at the upper levels of the organization. Maybe *it was decided* that a meeting *would be held.* Maybe so. But for God's and society's sakes, wouldn't it be nice if someone, somewhere would take the rap for deciding, denying, thinking, and developing?

Is anybody out there *doing* anything?

Or is it just *being done.*

A bad reputation, indeed. But we need not reflexively jerk our knees and abolish the passive voice. Certainly it *was developed* to satisfy some perceived need of human beings who wanted to communicate with each other. Assuredly, it didn't just arrive on the scene, the result of some dark conspiracy of briefcase-toting bureaucrats. It must have some redeeming social value.

It does. Eight, to be exact. At least I've been able to detect eight situations when the passive voice *is preferred.* Perhaps there are more. If you discover any, send me a letter and I'll give you credit in the next printing of this book. Promise.

**When the Passive Voice *Is Preferred***

1. When you are generalizing and you want to avoid using *one* as the subject of too many sentences.

   Active: Here are eight situations where one prefers the passive voice.

   Passive: Here are eight situations where the passive voice is preferred.

   Commentary: Let's face it, folks. One who uses lots of *ones* as the subjects of too many of one's sentences might indeed offend one's listeners or one's readers. One might even sound a bit snooty. Mightn't one? Translation: If too many *ones* are used, many readers and many listeners might be offended. Get it? Professors should get it. They are the worst offenders. In the faculty lounge (my, what goes on in there!), I once heard a professor ask: "Where might one find the coffee cream?" For heaven's sake, guys, try the passive: "Where is the coffee cream found?" Or better yet, forget the transitive verb *find* and inquire about the coffee cream's location. Go ahead. You can do it. Just use the verb *to be*: "Where in hell is the damn coffee cream?"

2. When the identity of the actor is the *punch* of the sentence and you want to place it at the end.

   Active: The President of the United States hid the tapes.

   Passive: The tapes were hidden by the President of the United States.

Commentary: This rule can work the other way as well. Sometimes the *beginning* of the sentence is the more emphatic place, as it is in a parallel *series* of sentences all opening with the same subject. If the punch is the recipient of the action, then passive voice constructions provide the only way to put recipients as grammatical subjects. See situation #8.

3. When the identity of the actor is irrelevant and you simply want to omit it.

   Active: The company established the policy in 1968.

   Passive: The policy was established in 1968.

4. When the identity of the actor is unknown.

   Active: Somebody mysteriously destroyed the files.

   Passive: The files were mysteriously destroyed.

5. When you want to hide the identity of the actor.

   Active: I regret to inform you that I misplaced your file.

   Passive: I regret to inform you that your file has been misplaced.

   Commentary: Seriously, you sometimes have to cover your, uh, self. However, let a healthy dollop of ethics restrict your use of situation #5.

6. When you want to avoid sexist writing but also want to avoid those horrible *s(he)'s*, *he/she's*, *him/her's*, and *his/her's*.

   Active: An applicant for employment must file his/her application with the personnel office. He/she should include his/her complete educational background.

   Passive: An application for employment must be filed with the personnel office. A complete educational background should be included.

   Commentary: Gross overreaction to the very real problem of sexist writing threatens the very foundations of our language. The problem is so vast that I've devoted Chapter 9 to a plague endangering every corner of the globe — his/hermaphrodism.

7. When the passive voice sounds better.

Active: A disreputable seller sometimes abuses and exploits consumers. (Too many sssssssss's!)

Passive: Consumers are sometimes abused and exploited by a disreputable seller.

Commentary: Watch out for this one. If you are a passive-voice addict in desperate need of your passive-voice fix every other sentence, then naturally the passive voice will always sound better to you. Test your writing. Search for and find the passive voice. Try the active. Get used to the active. Then, and only then, settle for the passive as the *better-sounding* construction.

8. When the recipient of the action is the subject matter of the rest of the paragraph.

Active: Smith, because he knows the workings of the Department, has lasted for more than a year. The President, nevertheless, probably will ask him to resign.

Passive: Smith, because he knows the workings of the Department, has lasted for more than a year. Nevertheless, he will probably be asked to resign.

Commentary: Here the focus is on Smith. He should be kept as the subject of the sentence.

Reread the previous sentence. Funny. This stuff really works.

**The Rules of Good Writing**

Your list of the rules of good writing now looks like this:

1. Use an average of 25 words per sentence.

2. Avoid putting too many messages in a single sentence.

3. Put most of your messages at the subject-predicate position.

4. For variety or emphasis, invert your sentences.

5. Use the art of subordination to smooth out choppiness.

6. Avoid disrupting your sentences with thought-stopping gaps.

7. Watch out for the rule of parallel construction.

8. Tabulate particularly complex information.

9. Hammer home your point with the powerful, versatile verb.

10. Use the verb *to be* only when you mean it.

11. Get rid of compound prepositions.

12. Cut adjective, adverb, and noun clauses to other structures satisfying the same functions.

13. Prefer the active voice, but use the passive to satisfy certain objectives concerning the identity or placement of the actor or recipient.

---

*Reference*

W. Strunk & E. White, *The Elements of Style* (3d ed. 1979).

# Chapter 8

## Losing Weight
## Miscellaneous Matters

*Proicit ampullas et sesquipedalia verba.*

Throws aside his paint-pots and his words a foot-and-a-half long.

—Horace

# Chapter 8

## Losing Weight

## Miscellaneous Matters

### Introduction

Every book has one of these chapters—a place for authors to put stuff that fits no where else. Kind of a boutique for the browser or shopper. Or a trash bin for the collector. Depends on your point of view.

In this chapter, in any event, I include a collection of dietary devices to help you trim down your writing. Lean writing is memorable. It wins arguments. Fat, ponderous writing is eminently forgettable. It typically loses. Much writing in business, government, and academe, though it seeks to inform and perhaps persuade, is usually ponderous and heavy, not lean and aggressive. By using the tricks we've discussed so far, enhanced by the miscellaneous matters in this chapter, you can achieve leanness in your writing. Then you'll be ready to write your way to the top.

### Long Words

Remember the passage of Justice Black's writing quoted in Chapter 1? Remember the passage from Justice Cardozo? In each of those passages, the writers used approximately 180 words. Also in each, two-thirds of the words were monosyllabic words. Simple, one-syllable words. Yet how many times have we made a beeline for our *Roget's* to find a longer word, a fancier word to express our meaning. Indeed, in college, trips to *Roget's* to find words no one knows—much less uses— were often awarded *A's* on term papers and book reports.

It's time to break those habits. It's time to learn to use short words. It's time to learn the power of short, Anglo-Saxon words. In report writing? In memos to the boss? In a term paper for a professor? Yes, in whatever you write. Black did it. Cardozo did it. So should you.

Fowler had a good time putting down those in love with long words.

In a most entertaining passage entitled *Love of the Long Word*, he urged us not to confuse "bulk with force":

> It need hardly be said that shortness is a merit in words. There are often reasons why shortness is not possible; much less often there are occasions when length, not shortness, is desirable. But it is a general truth that the short words are not only handier to use, but more *powerful* in effect; extra syllables reduce, not increase, vigour. This is particularly so in English, where the native words are short, and the long words are foreign. [Emphasis added.]
>
> . . . .
>
> Good English does consist in the main of short words. There are many good reasons, however, against any attempt to avoid a polysyllable if it is the word that will give our meaning best; moreover the occasional polysyllable will have added effect from being set among short words. What is here deprecated is the tendency among the ignorant to choose, because it is a polysyllable, the word that gives their meaning no better or even worse. (Fowler, pp. 344, 345).

Though I always get a feeling of country English tweed and a whiff of pipe smoke when I read Fowler, the man does have good opinions about our language. In a similar vein, Mr. E. B. White advised:

> Avoid the elaborate, the pretentious, the coy, and the cute. Do not be tempted by a twenty-dollar word when there is a ten-center handy, ready and able. Anglo-Saxon is a livelier tongue than Latin, so use Anglo-Saxon words. (Strunk & White, pp. 76-77).

Thus, consider the following translations of long words into short words. Notice the other devices used as well (denounification, passive voice obliteration, and clause-cutting):

| Long Word Style | Short Word Style |
| --- | --- |
| The record which has been compiled in the instant proceeding indicates that there is no evidence of any character or kind in support of the positions that have been claimed by the discharged employee. | The record in the current case shows no evidence whatsoever supporting the former employee's positions. |

Invocation of the above-mentioned principles of accounting will result in a reduction of losses that have been shown on the books of the company.

Using the above rules of accounting will dramatically reduce the paper losses of the company.

Changing long words to short words increases the vigor of your writing. Thus, don't say *indicates*, try *shows* instead. Don't say *invocation of*, try *using*. Changing long words to short words might even have a salutary effect on the clarity of your thinking.

Long words often are highly abstract. Because the meaning of abstractions might reside only in the reader or listener, long and abstract words often fail to pin down precise meaning. Another trick in making your writing leaner and meaner is preferring concrete words over abstract words.

### Favoring Concrete Words over Abstract Words

Concrete words create more vivid images. Consequently, concrete words carry more clout. In government, business, education, or law—all of which are already filled with so many abstract ideas—the careful writer will seek to use as many concrete words as possible, rather than heaping abstraction on abstraction. Why? Because concrete words will (are you ready?) staple your thoughts to your reader's mind. Good speech writers won't decry *hunger* in America. They'll speak instead of those eating dog food from a can. Good speech writers won't extol *opportunity* in America. They'll speak instead of the successful chocolate-chip cookie tycoon starting an empire from scratch. So too must good writers seek to grab the reader's attention with concrete images. Here, once again, is what Fowler had to say on the issue:

> Turgid flabby English is full of abstract nouns; the commonest ending of abstract nouns is *-ion*, and to count the *-ion* words in what one has written, or, better, to cultivate an ear that without special orders challenges them as they come, is one of the simplest and most effective means of making oneself less unreadable. It is as an unfailing sign of a nouny abstract style that a cluster of *-ion* words is chiefly to be dreaded. But some nouny writers are so far from being awake to that aspect of it that they fall into a still more obvious danger, and so stud their sentences

with *-ions* that the mere sound becomes an offence.... (Fowler, p. 640).

## Modification

While working for the Federal Judicial Center in Washington, D.C. during the late '70s, I watched an editor ply her trade with a report I was writing. She savagely ripped it to shreds, leaving behind a blood-like trail of red ink. Shrinking in horror, I asked, "What on earth are you doing?"

"Modification," was her terse reply.

"Who?"

She proceeded to show me how to pare down my language with a device called *modification*. Basically, the trick of modification derives from the effective use of adjectives and adverbs. Using modification is really quite simple. Search your writing for piles of words struggling to act as adjectives or adverbs. Find other, simpler, and often one-word adjectives and adverbs and use them instead. The device sometimes just repeats the trick of cutting clauses or destroying compound prepositions. Here's some simple modification:

| Before Modification | After Modification |
| --- | --- |
| the issues which were vital | the vital issues |
| trial by jury | jury trial |
| There are instances in which consumers are abused | Consumers are sometimes abused |

In the above examples, the writer recognized that the clause *which were vital* was trying to be a one-word adjective, that the prepositional phrase *by jury* could just as easily form a compound noun, and that the *there are instances in which* wanted to say *sometimes*. That's modification.

A few words of caution are in order. English is a remarkably versatile language. We can indeed change *legs of the chair* to *chair legs*. But watch out. When using modification, be careful you don't overdo it and use nouns as adjectives when perfectly good adjectives will do the job.

No one, for example, would arrange things in *alphabet order*. No. *Alphabetical order*. Know anybody who goes to *medicine school*? No.

*Medical school.* Thus, on your resume don't tout your *communication skills,* or you'll show your lack of them. Use the correct adjective. *Communicative skills.* If you misuse modification or overuse modification, you might then fall into the trap of . . .

### The Noun Modifier Proliferation Problem

If you overdo it, you might end up sounding like a page from the Pentagon Name Identification Procedure Manual Appendix. See the problem? These days, nouns used as modifiers have gotten completely out of control. Ironically, the device does derive from a genuine desire to be terse and pithy. (More likely it springs from the urge to produce a memorable acronym.) But if you use a whole slew of nouns to modify other nouns, you can create streams of words offending an ordinary sense of grace.

How far you cut down prepositional phrases is a judgment call. Thus, *judgment call* is a fairly well-recognized *compound noun* and doesn't overdo it. But *missile atmosphere reentry control system* is too modified. The way to smooth it out is to reinsert absent prepositional and verbal phrases: *system for controlling missiles reentering the atmosphere.*

### Do Not Tie Yourself Up In *Not's*

I just broke the rule. Let me follow it: *Try to avoid expressing negative conditions in negative terms.* It is awkward to use lots of *no's* and *not's.* Plenty of words in English can express the absence (there's one) of something without relying on awkward *no's* and *not's.* Thus, the *employee who is not present* is the *absent employee.* The *building that does not have adequate fire escapes* is the same one *that lacks adequate fire escapes.* If you *do not want to use too many negative expressions,* you might try *avoiding them.* Finally, if you *do not agree,* then you *disagree* or *dispute.*

Saying the negative without too many *no's* and *not's* always produces the more graceful style. Try it out. You'll like the result.

**The Rules of Good Writing**

Your list of the rules of good writing now looks like this:

1. Use an average of 25 words per sentence.
2. Avoid putting too many messages in a single sentence.
3. Put most of your messages at the subject-predicate position.
4. For variety or emphasis, invert your sentences.
5. Use the art of subordination to smooth out choppiness.
6. Avoid disrupting your sentences with thought-stopping gaps.
7. Watch out for the rule of parallel construction.
8. Tabulate particularly complex information.
9. Hammer home your point with the powerful, versatile verb.
10. Use the verb *to be* only when you mean it.
11. Get rid of compound prepositions.
12. Cut adjective, adverb, and noun clauses to other structures satisfying the same functions.
13. Prefer the active voice, but use the passive to satisfy certain objectives concerning the identity or placement of the actor or the recipient.
14. Favor short words over long, fancy words.
15. Use concrete words to staple your thoughts to your reader's mind.
16. Use modification to trim down the fat in your language.
17. Use phrases to smooth out the choppy noun-noun modifier.
18. Do not use too many negative expressions.

*References*

H. Fowler, *Modern English Usage* (2d ed. 1965).

W. Strunk & E. White, *The Elements of Style* (3d ed. 1979).

# Chapter 9

# His/hermaphrodism

*Multa renascentur quae iam cecidere, cadentque*
*Quae nunc sunt in honore vocabula, si volet usus,*
*Quem penes arbitrium est et ius et norma loquendi.*

Many terms that have now dropped out of favor will be revived,
and those that are at present respectable will drop out, if usage
so choose, with whom resides the decision and the judgment and
the code of speech.

—Horace

# Chapter 9

# His/hermaphrodism

## Introduction

Anyone who has ever written anything—especially recently—has faced the problem of his/hermaphrodism. You know the problem well. To be fair, you don't want to favor one sex over the other. To solve this problem of fairness, we seem to have developed a new gender, one that shares maleness and femaleness simultaneously, equally, and therefore fairly. We have, in short, created—out of nowhere—a his/hermaphrodite.

A writer will try to make a point about something. He or she needs an actor, yet because he or she is generalizing, he or she must pick a pronoun to convey his/her meaning. Sometimes (s)he will concoct all sorts of new words. Although these his/hermaphroditic expressions might sound fine to her/him, the reader can become somewhat confused about who is who. He or she isn't quite sure what he/she is trying to say to her or him. I mean the reader isn't sure what the writer is trying to say because the writer can't seem to decide whether he or she is a him or a her or a what.

There has to be a better way. In fact, there are three better ways. But before I get to the cures, let me make a lonely plea to preserve some of the grammar of the language.

## Agreement in Number—Agreement in Gender

Recall the use of personal pronouns. Also recall the *case* of personal pronouns (subjective, objective, and possessive) and the *number* of personal pronouns (singular and plural). Singular, third-person, personal pronouns include *he* and *she* in the subjective case, *him* and *her* in the objective case, and *his* and *her* in the possessive case. Obviously, each of these *singular* personal pronouns reveals gender. Plural, third-person, personal pronouns include *they* in the subjective case, *them* in the objective case, and *their* in the possessive case. Notice that *plural* pronouns do *not* reveal gender.

When you use a pronoun as a substitute for a noun, you typically reveal the noun first and then refer to that noun with a personal pronoun. Thus: *The girl (noun) announced her (pronoun) plans.* Or: *Tom Jackson (noun) announced his (pronoun) plans.* Or: *The manager (noun) announced her (pronoun) plans.* In the above sentences, *girl*, *Tom Jackson*, and *manager* are the *antecedents* of the later pronouns. Because in each case the writer knows the sex of *girl*, *Tom Jackson*, and *manager*, the writer can use the correct pronouns in the correct *gender*. Also, because each antecedent is singular, the writer can use the correct pronouns in the correct *number* to restate those singular nouns—those singular antecedents.

One of the cardinal rules of grammar—and, with a little effort, it can remain so—requires that a singular pronoun refer to a singular antecedent and a plural pronoun refer to a plural antecedent. Thus, you would not say: *The manager announced their plans.* If you did, your meaning would totally change. The manager doesn't solely possess a set of plans. Rather, she jointly owns some plans with at least one other person, whose identity remains a mystery.

The problem of his/hermaphrodism arises when the writer is generalizing (as I am now generalizing about a *writer*). If I later refer to this writer as *he*, I unfairly exclude girls and women from the generalized class of writers. And if I later refer to this writer as *she*, I unfairly exclude boys and men from the class as well. Reacting to an overwhelming urge to be fair, the writer succumbs to his/hermaphrodism and proceeds to botch up his or her writing with lots of extra words that might obscure his or her meaning.

One thing a writer might do to wreak havoc on the language is break the rule of *number agreement*. A writer might use a singular antecedent and then use plural pronouns when they later want to refer to that singular antecedent. The writer forgets that their reader will lose faith in them if they insist on referring to a previously identified, singular antecedent with a later plural pronoun. All in the name of fairness— thus do we tear our language apart.

Before getting to some solutions to this very real dilemma, I should point out one recognized exception to the *number agreement* rule. Many times in writing, someone will use an *indefinite* pronoun. They may then follow that singular, indefinite pronoun with a later plural pronoun. Reread the last two sentences, and you'll see the rule in action. *Someone* is an indefinite pronoun. It is also singular. Rules of grammar permit a plural pronoun to restate a singular antecedent when that antecedent itself is an *indefinite pronoun*. Hence, the word *they* is correctly used to refer to the singular *someone*. Indefinite pronouns include: *someone, anyone, each, one, everyone,* and some others. Thus, it is correct to say: *Anyone may bring their lunch.* It is also correct to say: *Everyone is entitled to their own opinion.*

### The Problem

Here's the problem:

> An applicant for employment must file his or her application with the personnel office. He/she should include his/her educational background, a listing of three of his/her references, and a summary of his/her employment experience.

### The Plural Antecedent Solution

One very easy solution to the problem is to make your antecedents plural. Typically, you'll be generalizing about *an applicant, a writer,* or *a taxpayer.* It's quite easy to say the same things about *applicants, writers,* or *taxpayers.* When you do, you have the plural pronouns readily available. And, of most importance, *they, their,* and *them* do not discriminate on the basis of sex. Watch it work:

> Applicants for employment must file their applications with the personnel office. They should include their educational backgrounds, listings of three of their references, and summaries of their employment experience.

A word of caution. Writers should use their heads when using this approach. After all, writers have *heads*—plural—just as *applicants* have *applications, backgrounds, listings,* and *summaries.* When the antecedent is plural, take care to make all succeeding elements plural.

### The Passive Voice Solution

You learned in Chapter 8 to manipulate the voice of transitive verbs to achieve certain objectives. One of those objectives was to avoid sexist writing. By using the passive voice, you obviate the need to reveal actors. Hiding the identity of the actors also hides their sex. Discriminatory writing disappears as well:

An application for employment must be filed with the personnel office. An educational background, a listing of three references, and a summary of employment experience should be included.

## The Second-Person Pronoun Solution

We can thank the Department of the Navy's Office of the Judge Advocate General for this solution. While teaching my writing course to attorneys in Washington, I received this suggestion from a Navy attorney: use the second-person pronoun when your writing is instructional. The second-person pronoun, he correctly pointed out, is not gender-based.

To apply for employment, file an application with the personnel office. You should include an educational background, a listing of three of your references, and a summary of your employment experience.

Bingo. His/hermaphrodism loses. The language wins.

## The Pick-a-Pronoun Solution

Sometimes these three solutions just won't work. The passive voice is just too wimpy, plural antecedents don't sound right, or second-person pronouns are out of place. In that case, use *he or she* if the occurrence is infrequent and doesn't get out of control. Otherwise, pick *he* or *she* and use it consistently.

Combating his/hermaphrodism is certainly worth the effort. Being fair is worth the effort, too. By fighting to preserve the language while simultaneously promoting fairness, you can justifiably look upon yourself as one of the English language's most steadfast spokesindividuals. By all means, be fair. But don't be stupid.

## The Rules of Good Writing

At last, your list of the rules of good writing looks like this:

1. Use an average of 25 words per sentence.
2. Avoid putting too many messages in a single sentence.
3. Put most of your messages at the subject-predicate position.
4. For variety or emphasis, invert your sentences.
5. Use the art of subordination to smooth out choppiness.
6. Avoid disrupting your sentences with thought-stopping gaps.
7. Watch out for the rule of parallel construction.
8. Tabulate particularly complex information.
9. Hammer home your point with the powerful, versatile verb.
10. Use the verb *to be* only when you mean it.
11. Get rid of compound prepositions.
12. Cut adjective, adverb, and noun clauses to other structures satisfying the same functions.
13. Prefer the active voice, but use the passive to satisfy certain objectives concerning the identity or placement of the actor or the recipient.
14. Favor short words over long, fancy words.
15. Use concrete words to staple your thoughts to your reader's mind.
16. Use modification to trim down the fat in your language.
17. Use phrases to smooth out the choppy noun-noun modifier.
18. Do not use too many negative expressions.
19. Be fair and nonsexist, but don't be stupid.

That's all there is to it. I'll try to tie it all together in some final, parting shots on matters of style.

# Chapter 10

# Some Parting Shots
# on Matters of Style

*Et semel emissum volat irrevocabile verbum.*

And once sent out, a word takes wing irrevocably.

—Horace

# Chapter 10

## Some Parting Shots

## on Matters of Style

What makes good writing good and bad writing bad? Here's the "final" list of the rules of good writing:

1. Use an average of 25 words per sentence.
2. Avoid putting too many messages in a single sentence.
3. Put most of your messages at the subject-predicate position.
4. For variety or emphasis, invert your sentences.
5. Use the art of subordination to smooth out choppiness.
6. Avoid disrupting your sentences with thought-stopping gaps.
7. Watch out for the rule of parallel construction.
8. Tabulate particularly complex information.
9. Hammer home your point with the powerful, versatile verb.
10. Use the verb *to be* only when you mean it.
11. Get rid of compound prepositions.
12. Cut adjective, adverb, and noun clauses to other structures satisfying the same functions.
13. Prefer the active voice, but use the passive to satisfy certain objectives concerning the identity or placement of the actor or the recipient.
14. Favor short words over long, fancy words.
15. Use concrete words to staple your thoughts to your reader's mind.
16. Use modification to trim down the fat in your language.
17. Use phrases to smooth out the choppy noun-noun modifier.
18. Do not use too many negative expressions.
19. Be fair and nonsexist, but don't be stupid.

## The Rules of Good Writing

To write powerfully—to wield your mighty sword—you must pay attention to sentence structure. You've got to know that sentences typically appear in one of four forms. They will consist of a subject plus transitive verb plus object, subject plus intransitive verb plus adverb, subject plus *to be* plus adjective, subject plus *to be* plus noun, or subject plus linking verb plus adjective. From these basic structures comes the first rule of style: Keep your sentences short. Your reader is not too excited about sticking with one of your sentences for more than 25 words. To grab your reader's attention and not let go, keep your sentences short and to the point. Second, dish out your messages a bite at a time. Avoid putting too many messages in one grammatical sentence. Third, your reader fully expects to find your main message placed at the strategic part of your sentences. Let your subject and your main verb carry most of your messages. Vary that approach only for emphasis or variety. Fourth, when you tire of straightforward writing, flip your sentences with the art of inversion. Fifth, if you carry these rules to the extreme, your writing will be too short and choppy. Develop an ear for those sentences crying out for subordination. Learn to weave the information in one sentence into another nearby. Recognize situations calling for subordinate clauses, prepositional phrases, verbal phrases, or appositive phrases. Sixth, remember to keep strategic parts of your sentences close together. Keep subject next to verb, verb next to object, and complex-verb words next to one another. In short, avoid gaps. Seventh, remember those extraordinarily important conjunctions—the coordinating and correlative conjunctions. Your readers expect them to join equal grammatical units, so keep your writing parallel. Also remember to use the notion of parallel construction as a way not only to identify those constructions you use but to uncover those constructions missing from your written language. When was the last time you used a correlative conjunction to join two infinitive phrases? I just did. Three sentences ago. It works. After all, parallelism helped me write this book. The eighth and final trick to fine-tune your sentences is the device of tabulation. Go ahead and make lists in your writing, but be sure to follow rules of grammar and style in making those lists. Do all these things to your sentences and your writing will improve.

Then turn your attention to your words. The ninth item on our list of the rules of good writing is perhaps the most important of all.

Denounification. The mere sound of the word alone should prove the worth of the goal it seeks. Unstuff your language. Cut out those piles of pillowy nouns. Bare your fists with hard-hitting, action-packed verbs. That's the way to win the battle of words in class or on the job. Or anywhere else. Tenth, learn to use the verb *to be* only when you really mean it. If you're a part of the "new generation," pay special attention to your language. *Like, go, waslike,* and other parts of nonspeech threaten thought itself. Really and truly, you'll go nowhere talking and thinking that way. Eleventh, declare war on compound prepositions. They really are quite tyrannical, never fessing up with respect to their precise meaning. Twelfth, watch out for clauses. Too many of them inevitably get in the way of clear writing. Learn to substitute true nouns or gerunds for nominal clauses. Learn to replace adjective or adverb clauses with verbal phrases, prepositional phrases, one-word adjectives or adverbs, adjective appositives, truncated adverb clauses, and absolutes. Thirteenth, as a rule, you should prefer the active voice over the passive voice. If the majority of your sentences appear in the passive voice, no subject ever does anything. All subjects just sit there and take it. Your writing, in the passive voice, will lack a sense of activity, a sense of urgency. Your writing, in the passive voice, will just be weak and wimpy. Not exactly a prescription for victory. Fourteenth, use short words. They always do a better job than long ones, even in term papers or memos to the boss. And, yes, in scholarly journals. Especially in scholarly journals. Fifteenth, concrete words usually paint more vivid images in the reader's mind. Though many professions must necessarily deal with abstractions, using concrete words to express or exemplify those abstract doctrines will do much to staple your thoughts to your reader. Sixteenth, you can put your writing on a diet by using the device of modification to trim out excess verbiage. Useless clauses and prepositional phrases can often be replaced by one-word adjectives and adverbs. Seventeenth, keep modification within reasonable bounds. Don't overdo it and produce long-winded chains of nouns used as adjectives. Eighteenth, avoid negative expressions. That says it just fine. And lastly, nineteenthly, please keep our language. It has done a good job for so long. The language, the ear, and good sense recoil at *he/she's* and *s(he)'s.*

That's the way to write. Learn these rules of grammar and a good, powerful style will necessarily follow. The rules of grammar, after all, didn't just pop up overnight. They didn't just materialize out of your eighth-grade grammar book. Your teachers didn't just make them up to trip you up. They rule the language—these rules of grammar. They rule the language that conveys our thoughts. Without them, we can't talk, we can't write. Indeed, without them, we can't even think. So use these rules of grammar. They aren't really leering over your shoulder waiting to pounce on your slightest error.

They are, instead, your weapons in whatever battles you must fight with words.

The End

*Nunc est bibendum, nunc pede libero Pulsanda tellus.*

Now for drinks, now for some dancing with a good beat.

—Horace